CW01471770

The Covert Narcissist

Recognizing the Most Dangerous and Subtle Form of Emotional Manipulation and Recovering from Abuse

Bianca Sutton

©Copyright 2021 – Bianca Sutton - All rights reserved

The content contained within this book may not be reproduced, duplicated, or transmitted without direct written permission from the author or the publisher.

Under no circumstances will any blame or legal responsibility be held against the publisher, or author, for any damages, reparation, or monetary loss due to the information contained within this book, either directly or indirectly.

Legal Notice

This book is copyright protected. This book is only for personal use. You cannot amend, distribute, sell, use, quote, or paraphrase any part, or the content within this book, without the consent of the author-publisher.

Disclaimer Notice

Please note the information contained within this document is for educational and entertainment purposes only. All effort has been executed to present accurate, up-to-date, and reliable, complete information. No warranties of any kind are declared or implied. Readers acknowledge that the author is not engaging in the rendering of legal, financial, medical, or professional advice.

Table of Contents

Introduction

Both narcissists and co-workers with an antisocial personality disorder (often incorrectly referred to as sociopaths) tend to be manipulative and lack empathy for others. They are both exploitative. While a sociopath represses empathy to avoid rejection, the covert narcissist represses it because he lacks self-esteem.

Narcissists are primarily concerned with their own needs and desires, while co-workers who have an antisocial personality disorder are mainly worried about others' needs. The covert narcissist has low self-esteem and fears that others will reject or humiliate him if he shows his true feelings. He is hiding himself to preserve his narcissistic façade of perfection despite his lack of an actual model of normalcy.

This condition is often apparent to others who are wise enough to understand what a narcissist truly is but tolerant enough not to confront the person about it. It is also evident to insiders, as they recognize the lack of essential regard for other people while avoiding confrontation for fear of negative consequences. Insiders may choose not to attempt to change the person, fearing he will become angry and violent towards them or dismiss his grandiose delusions entirely. Insiders might get hurt or lose their jobs in the process.

Covert narcissists often leave their co-workers and friends under the impression that they are well-liked and generally well-respected because of their strength of character, leadership abilities, and ease in making difficult decisions. However, in reality, they are very manipulative and controlling. They will often keep secrets from others about their true character and their need for validation. At their worst, they can even throw one person under the bus while throwing everyone else under too, except themselves, out of frustration and anger, leading him to become more violent towards even those he is closest to.

Chapter 1:
Origins of a Narcissist

D id you know that the term, narcissist, originates from Greek mythology? As the story goes, Narcissus, a very handsome man, disregarded the offers and advances of Echo, a nymph. As his punishment, he was cursed to love his image excessively in a pool of water. Gazing upon his reflection in the water for the first time, he felt utmost adoration, and he could no longer stop. Sadly, he was unable to enjoy nor consummate his love for himself. As Narcissus pined and yearned for a consumable love, he changed into a beautiful flower that bore his name, the narcissus.

The concept of self-adoration dates back to the early philosophers and psychologists in ancient history. In earlier Greek times, narcissism was thought to be hubris, defined as the state of extreme arrogance and haughtiness. Much later, philosophers in the 1900s further described it as being out of touch with reality when narcissism started to flourish in the budding school of thought known as psychoanalysis. Otto Rank, an Austrian psychoanalyst, was the first to publish a description of narcissism in 1911. In his studies, he connected narcissism with self-adoration and vanity.

Sigmund Freud furthered Rank's research in 1914 when he published a paper entitled, "Narcissism: An Introduction." Freud suggested that narcissism is associated with one's libido or the energy that drives a person to survive. According to Freud, an infant has innate selfishness because his libido is directed inward, a condition known as primary narcissism. Among babies, this condition is natural because they cannot do anything to acquire their needs but must rely on their primary caregivers or mothers. However, as the child comes of age, he starts to fend for himself. In turn, the libido shifts its direction outwards, relying on the adult's attachment of others. As a baby, he is used to being the center of attention – in the family's life. As he grows up, he realizes that this attention diminishes over time. This outward extension of the libido craves the affection of other people. It involves receiving love, care, admiration, and an appraisal from family and friends.

Sigmund Freud added that a child develops a self-image when he starts to interact with his environment. He begins to learn about social norms and cultural expectations. He conceptualizes an ideal image to pursue and attain. An essential key point from Freud's study is the idea that self-love and self-adoration may be transferred to other human beings or things. By giving away love, a person starts to diminish his primary narcissism, making him feel more vulnerable and leaving him less able to nurture and protect himself from several environmental factors. To replenish this security, Freud theorized that a person starts to feel secure and protected against all elements that aim to reduce his integrity by receiving love and affection.

It was not until the 1950s and 1960s that narcissism was classified as a disorder. During this time, Otto Kernberg and Heinz Kohut worked to shed more light on the concept. In 1967, Kernberg constructed the "narcissistic personality structure" and classified narcissism into three major types: normal adult narcissism, normal infantile narcissism (primary narcissism according to Freud), and pathological narcissism.

Finally, in 1968, Kohut understood more about the narcissistic personality disorder and took some of Sigmund Freud's ideas to support his theory. Narcissism then became a vital tool in "Self-Psychology," which suggests that narcissism is a normal part of early development. Kohut also theorized that a person's challenges and difficulties during his early "self-object" relationships affect his self-esteem later in life, leading to narcissistic disorders. It was not until 1980 that Narcissistic Personality Disorder (NPD) was born as an official diagnosis of this mental anomaly.

Narcissism is defined as having an excessive admiration of the self. Psychology describes the term as a deep sense of interest in the self-characterized by a lack of empathy. Narcissists are often characterized by high self-worth. This affects the thoughts and behaviors of an individual, as well as his interaction with others.

It is always easy to identify a narcissistic person in a group of people. Such individuals always excite the crowd and keep sharing stories about themselves. Narcissists tend to be manipulated and often lack a sense of compassion. Other traits associated with this personality include:

· I crave appreciation and acknowledgement, even when nothing has been accomplished.

· Appreciation of personal beauty and success.

· A feeling of being better than others.

· Exploitation and manipulation of others.

· Grandiosity and a high emphasis on self.

· Fantasies of being critical, famous or influential.

· Exaggeration of individual accomplishments and abilities.

Narcissistic Personality Disorder

Narcissistic personality disorder or NPD is a mental condition that makes people place more importance on themselves. The disorder is known to cause problematic relationship since patients often suffer from low self-esteem. It also causes issues at work, school and any other situation where collaboration is required.

Narcissists keep getting disappointed and unhappy when they are not given enough attention. Other people find it difficult to spend time around them because they always want to be pampered even when they do not deserve it.

Symptoms of the disorder include:

· High self-importance

This is one of the significant characteristics of NPD. It results in a high feeling of superiority, which often comes out as arrogance. Individuals with this disorder tend to believe that they are exceptional in some way and no one can understand them. They do not settle for average things since their standards are set too high. Therefore, they only associate with high-profile events, places and individuals. Because narcissists believe they are more important than others, they always demand to be recognized even when they have achieved nothing.

Narcissists are experts at fabricating lies and exaggerating situations just to get attention. They will never speak positively about others, even when an achievement results from a team effort. They make people feel indebted to them at all times.

· Fantasy

Narcissists are never absolute. They develop a world built on deception and imaginary thoughts. They create an atmosphere that glorifies them and does not consider themselves as failures. They love being in power and enjoy places where they are given total control. Such a world shields them from being ashamed about the reality of their lives.

Narcissists do not take criticism positively. Most ignore opinions and facts contrary to their beliefs. Any information or action that resists their fantasy is always treated with anger and defensiveness. Because they live in denial, it becomes difficult for others to create meaningful relationships with narcissistic people.

· Craving for admiration

To become good friends with a narcissist, you will need to praise him for every minor achievement - constantly. Individuals with this disorder survive on recognition and praise. That is why most of them surround themselves with individuals ready to shower them with glory and affirmation all the time.

· Feeling of entitlement

Due to their self-centeredness, individuals with narcissistic personality disorder keep expecting nothing but favors from others. They always get what they need. When associating with such a person, you must comply with their every demand. You are considered useless if you cannot do as instructed by the narcissist. If you do not comply, you will receive nothing except rage and ill-treatment in return.

· Exploitation

Narcissistic individuals can never connect with your feelings. It is almost impossible for them to identify with your pain or happiness.

They can never put themselves in your shoes. Instead, they only manipulate you to get what they need. They see you as their servant, not the other way round. They will always take advantage of your availability to meet their needs. Narcissists never reflect on their behavior and how it can affect their relationship with others.

· Intimidation

If you are a person who fears getting intimidated, you cannot work with a narcissist. Narcissists can never get along with you if you seem to be more popular and talented. If you dare challenge any of them, you will be met with a high level of defensiveness. They will do everything just to make you appear inferior. If this does not work, they will end up insulting you or retreating from your presence altogether.

You need to understand that people with the narcissistic disorder can appear to be very charming. They always succeed in creating a very positive self-image. They come across as confident all the time and can easily lure you into believing in their fantasies. When dealing with them, you need to understand what they are looking for – admirers. Do not expect to receive any special treatment. You should treat a selfish person just as he is. To assist the person, you need to stop defending his lousy behavior.

· Setting helpful boundaries

Kindness and respect are some of the factors that characterize good relationships. One weakness narcissists struggle with is the inability to reciprocate kindness. They are unable to recognize others with importance because their needs always come first. To overcome this, they need to identify and set proper boundaries when dealing with other people. If you are a narcissist seeking to recover from the disorder, you need to highlight those things that violate your respect for others and deal with them accordingly.

· Learn to consider the feelings of others

Recovering from the NPD requires that you identify where the focus on self needs to end. It would help if you appreciated the existence of others by being aware of their feelings and thoughts. You can do this by:

· Speaking cautiously to others. When addressing them, call them by their names.

· Avoid talking too much. As much as you have a lot to share, it would be best to allow others to speak.

· Show interest in the affairs of others. Ask questions that make you appear concerned about the welfare of other people.

· Keep out of other people's space. Do not use their items or time without permission.

· Deliver substance

To reduce the anxiety and stress associated with the disorder, make sure that you deliver on your assignments. Doing this will eliminate the need to lie or exaggerate the results to gain appreciated. You will also get to enjoy healthier relationships built around friendship and trust. Some of the practical things you can do to achieve this include:

· Doing exactly what you promise. Keep your promises when it comes to appointments and agreements.

· Do not overpromise. It is better to under-promise and over-deliver.

· Take responsibility for any failures. Be accountable for the mistakes you make.

· Concentrate on impacting others differently. Do not engage in activities that will jeopardize your integrity. Also, avoid decisions that will make others feel manipulated and cheated.

Causes of Narcissism

Just as with many other disorders, the primary cause of narcissistic personality disorder remains unknown. However, it is believed that the condition arises due to specific childhood encounters, genetics, and psychological factors. Most people learn narcissistic traits from their seniors when growing up. Such features become difficult to stop and later develop into a disorder.

Some of the risk factors experienced in childhood that may trigger the disorder are:

· Having insensitive parents.

· Excessive pampering, praise and admiration with parents and other family members.

· Negligence when it comes to childhood care.

· Parents that over criticize their children.

· Childhood trauma and abuse.

· High-performance expectations from parents and family members

The disorder also occurs when the genes connecting behavior to the brain develop abnormally.

Narcissism and Society

Narcissism has existed for several decades. However, the concept has become rampant in the modern world as more cases are being reported every day.

Narcissists are masters at ignoring their limitations. Since they love themselves too much, they tend to live in illusion and self-deception to avoid facing reality. They do this by creating a false image of themselves clouded by numerous fantasies. Their true identity is hidden behind a mask that is not easy to identify. In reality, narcissists are suffering individuals who need a lot of assistance and understanding. As they continue to avoid reality, they develop a strong defense strategy that is difficult to overcome.

Although only a few narcissism cases get to the point a real disorder, almost every human being has at least one narcissistic tendency. It is a survival mechanism used to compensate for failures and shortcomings. People use it together with self-deception to avoid circumstances that lead to shame. It helps people overcome depression since most narcissists do not love themselves. Their narcissistic behavior helps them cover up their deep sense of inferiority and self-hatred.

Narcissists always project themselves as highly intelligent, eloquent and gifted. This projection comes out as arrogance and pride. They want the world to know how important they are. Their intention is never to hurt anyone, but their actions and feelings end up as emotional trauma for others. They feel no remorse for causing harm and may justify themselves to get out of awkward situations. Their main distinction is the lack of concern for their environment. They never bother about their actions and how they may affect their relationships. It is one way of getting attention from the world.

Narcissists are always indifferent towards the progress of others. They only get involved in activities that satisfy them. Their interest in other people's affairs is never genuine unless there is a platform for exercising their superiority. A good number of con artists in the world are selfish. Since they are deceptive, it is easy for them to con others and get away with it. Life becomes painful for them when they cannot achieve their selfish desires. They love it when people fear them.

A narcissistic person will change his personality or self-image based on the admiration he wants to receive from others. He will view himself through other people's eyes and then create a fake image that replaces what he sees. In reality, this image does not exist. A narcissist can assume a lifestyle that is not his just to remain in the limelight.

Narcissism is experienced everywhere. Narcissists can be your colleagues, family members or acquaintances. When it comes to the workplace, awareness must be created due to the arrogance and bullying nature of narcissism. By nature, selfishness remains a big challenge for organizations given the negative impact it causes on individual and team performance. Narcissistic workmates fail to realize the need for help. They will frustrate their colleagues and feel good when they get others into trouble.

When in the workplace, it is easy to identify a colleague with narcissistic traits. He or she will tend to:

· Inflate his ego and always force his way within the work environment.

· Never admit he is wrong even when a team has made a mistake.

· He will consider any mistake as someone else's fault.

· The narcissist will use mind control tactics to win other colleagues to his side. He may use the same technique to beat his boss.

Chapter 2:
The Covert Narcissist

C overt narcissists can be described as narcissists who don't fit into a narcissist's stereotypical personality profile. Covert narcissism may be more challenging to spot in several ways because of the narcissist's introverted character. Though it's just as dangerous as its extroverted counterpart, covert narcissism is a more hidden form of abuse and can be trickier to pinpoint.

The main thing a covert narcissist has in common with an extroverted one is that they both use superiority to cover their internal vulnerability. This, in turn, is also used to make their victim feel insecure or off-balance about themselves or the situation. While some narcissists might outright say, "I'm better than you, so play by my rules," a covert narcissist will instead strongly hint at it. They won't be direct about it, but you'll still feel the same degradation as if they'd said it directly.

While they may not display all the characteristics or behaviors outlined, a covert narcissist will demonstrate some of the following throughout their relationship with you. You may find that the covert narcissist in your life displays several of these traits or they only show them from time to time. Regardless, these ways of behaving should act as a warning, at the very least, and offer you the ability to spot when you've become the victim of a narcissist.

· Smugness

Being quietly observant, judgmental and showing gestures of superiority are characteristics you'll find in a covert narcissist. They tend to act with an air of smugness, which can leave you feeling belittled, confused, and often like you're simply not good enough.

When you're talking or taking "center stage" in a social setting, or even if it's just you and them, they will offer distant and uninterested behavior. However, when they're speaking, you may find that as well as the conversation being focusing on them and their views, they'll also attempt to belittle you and your opinions. Their critical, judgmental comments are, of course, very hurtful and humiliating.

· Highly Sensitive

Covert narcissists tend to handle criticism, or perceived criticism, very poorly. They deem negative feedback or constructive criticism as a personal attack on them. They react in one of two ways: they get highly defensive and use the smug superiority described above to dismiss any unwanted feedback, or they will sulkily withdraw from the situation.

Typically, a covert narcissist won't tell you outright what is bothering them, but instead they will let their cold behavior towards you let you know that something is up.

· Passive-Aggressiveness

Passive-aggressiveness in a covert narcissist can in becoming angry and hostile, and they'll often offer fake helpfulness with no intention of ever helping you. These passive-aggressive behaviors are expressed in covert ways, giving the narcissist an underhanded advantage over the situation. If an undercover narcissist feels threatened, they'll use passive-aggressive behavior to ensure they control the problem. These passive-aggressive tactics are a stealthy way to punish those who dare to hurt their fragile egos.

With a covert narcissist, this passive aggression will offer a thinly disguised sense of superiority, entitlement, and an unintentional way to showcase their arrogant view of the world. A covert narcissist is inclined to become hostile if they don't get their way. Even if their requests or demands are unreasonable, they'll devise stealthy yet destructive ways to make you miserable for hurting their delicate sense of entitlement.

Some examples of passive-aggressiveness include:

Verbal hostility: For a covert narcissist, putting other people down makes them feel self-assured and superior. This allows them to seek and obtain a false sense of importance, and their critical and hostile way of speaking to you will fuel their narcissistic fire.

In a nutshell, passive-aggressive verbal hostility from the narcissist is their habitual criticism of your ideas, experiences and feelings.

Hostile humor: Very thinly-veiled hostile banter or joking is often followed by the phrases, "I was just kidding" or "can't you take a joke?" Sarcastic, feisty humor offered by a covert narcissist is their way of expressing their internal anger, rejection or disapproval towards you.

Blaming: Blaming is a form of gaslighting for which narcissists are renowned. The intention behind the blameful behavior is to avoid any responsibility by manipulating the facts of the situation. A covert narcissist will distort your perception of a problem or conversation, therefore making it easier to place blame elsewhere. Often the undercover narcissist will misdirect the blame onto you, thus refocusing away from the real issue at hand: their failures and bad behavior.

Covert Sabotage: Covert sabotage is the narcissist's way of sneakily administering punishment on you in a very disguised way. Examples of this could be the narcissist deliberately disclosing hurtful and harmful information or deliberately obstructing positive endeavors or communications. Other examples could be the narcissist deliberately undermining any agreements you've made with them. The narcissist could also purposely overspend your agreed upon budget, this causing you financial difficulty - but of course, you'd be the person who gets handed the blame for this.

· Lack of Empathy

A distinct lack of empathy is a trait the covert narcissist shares with an extroverted narcissist. Both narcissist types are so self-absorbed and self-serving that they are dismissive of other people's feelings. Often, their apparent dismissiveness of your thoughts and feelings is, in fact, complete obliviousness to your senses.

Frustratingly, even when you tell the narcissist that their behavior or attitude is upsetting you or it'll result in dire consequences, their response will often be reverted back to them. Your needs, wants, thoughts, and feelings aren't the narcissist's main priority.

· the "I'm Special" Complex

A covert narcissist, although introverted, can still have a "special person" complex. They may heavily hint at being misunderstood, almost like they're so evolved that nobody can understand their genius or uniqueness. This "special person" complex is something the covert narcissist uses as a "woe is me" story: they may claim they feel isolated and misunderstood because they're so one-of-a-kind that nobody understands them.

Of course, this complex is just another way for the narcissist to bury his vulnerable and fearful true self.

· Impersonal Relationships

Covert narcissists are deeply insecure about their inability to connect with people in a meaningful way. They want to avoid being exposed for their interpersonal inadequacies and hide their incapability to forge deep relationships with others.

· Self-Absorbed

Self-centeredness and self-absorption are general characteristics of a covert narcissist. These introverted narcissists are destitute listeners and, as such, they form quick opinions on people and situations.

Quiet people are widely assumed to be good listeners, although this isn't the case; the opposite is true. Because of their self-absorption, they often find things that aren't about them (or things that will directly affect them) uninteresting and unworthy of their attention.

It's ironic that self-absorbed people, like the covert narcissist, also lack the self-awareness that the rest of us possess. While we are fortunate to have the ability to reflect on our actions and behavior, the narcissist is unable (or unwilling in a lot of cases) to fully recognize just how self-absorbed he is.

Most of us recognize the nuances of situations and understand that not everything always goes our way. However, covert narcissists generally only focus on their wants and, selfishly, what they deem to be agreeable. Anything else is uninteresting or a waste of time.

Hopefully, the above explanations have helped you understand what a covert narcissist is, and now you have some idea of the behaviors and characteristics that outline this type of narcissist. While this helps illuminate one type of abuse, pinpointing when you're the victim of a narcissist can be pretty hard to do, especially without guidance.

It's important to remember that the covert narcissist is possibly the most complicated type of abuse to spot. Generally, they look for highly empathetic people who will listen to their sob stories and give the narcissist the benefit of the doubt. Once the victim begins to feel a sense of responsibility for their narcissistic partner, and that's when the abuser knows they have them reeled in and they amp up their abuse in the relationship.

The victim is then trapped in a vicious cycle. Over time, the covert narcissist will make the victim question their perception of reality, doubt themselves, and accept blame readily. Because of this, the narcissist ensures that they won't be held accountable for their behavior by the victim.

As with all narcissists, covert narcissists do have a predictable behavior pattern for romantic partners. In the beginning, they may appear to idealize their partners. This acts as bait for their victims. Once the victim is hooked in, the narcissist will then devalue their partner, and (as you sadly may be all too aware), this causes the victim to chase the love and adoration they received from their abuser previously.

The victim is unaware that this devaluation from the abuser is done with sinister and purposeful intent. After this, the narcissist will then discard their partner.

The covert narcissist may appear as a calm, quiet and polite person to most people. However, when you're in a relationship with one, they're often cold, distant, abusive and demeaning. Jekyll and Hyde can be a good way of describing their personality and treatment of you.

Often, a covert narcissist is seemingly quiet and can usually be described as meek and inoffensive by most people, but behind closed doors, it can be a very different story. They thrive on their partners' failures and upset. It's not an uncommon game for a covert narcissist to set you up for loss or upset. The crazy-making thing about this is that the narcissist will then punish you for failure. Introverted narcissists are also renowned for making empty promises without ever having any intention of delivering. They will then get a twisted kick out of your reaction when they fail to provide, often making themselves appear as the victim and making you look unreasonable and selfish with unbearable expectations.

A hurtful and frustrating aspect to this behavior of making promises without delivering is when the narcissist will deny ever making that promise in the first place. This gaslighting behavior often makes you think you're losing your mind and makes you question your perception of reality. This is known as "perceptive*".

The best way to describe a covert narcissist's internal feeling would be "conflicted". While the narcissist wants to be worshipped and adored, and they think quite a lot of themselves, they are also incredibly insecure. This internal conflict creates the unbalanced, manipulative and willful confidence-sucker that is the covert narcissist.

Chapter 3:
Am I a Narcissist?

N arcissistic tendencies are always problematic, but there are times when it is worse than others. A "healthy" dose of narcissism can be beneficial. It is defined as having self-esteem while still maintaining a connection to others. It is self-love without being detrimental to others.

However, this isn't always the case. Sometimes narcissistic tendencies are extreme and need some profound changes. If this is something you fear might be affecting you or someone in your life, please read on for more information.

Sociopath

A sociopath is someone who is usually defined by a lack of empathy. Someone with an antisocial personality is often seen as a sociopath as they do not interact with others because people without this form of narcissism do. They're known for being very charming and likeable, but this is all a façade. Underneath all of that superficial falseness, they're calculating and have controlling behavior.

Here is a list of an indication to look out for:

· Being deceitful and lying. For example, they might con others and feel no remorse or use an alias to hide or what they're doing.

· An inability to follow social norms. They may act in inappropriate ways, from speaking out of turn to breaking the law.

· Overly assertive or aggressive behavior. It may be prone to getting into physical fights.

· An absence of empathy for others' feelings, even if they are responsible for those feelings.

· A display of very shallow feelings

· Impulsive behavior that hinders planning for the future.

· Lack of concern for others' safety.

· Irresponsibility that drives inconsistent behavior

· Taking part in reckless behavior, such as stealing, promiscuity, and taking uncalculated risks.

This behavior is worrying because it can lead to abusive relationships, aggression, and even violence. The longer people allow it to continue, the worse it will get. The further a sociopath will push the boundaries to see what they can get away with. It needs to be allocated right away to protect everyone who comes into contact with this person.

If you happen to identify with this list or know someone who shows no remorse for their actions, no matter what they've done, and they don't recognize that they need to change, then they might be a narcissistic sociopath. Studies have shown this often emanates from neglecting parents, sociopathic parents, or traumatic, abusive events. It can best be treated with a medical professional's help, and it's usually done via therapy.

Psychopath

Before this study, it has always been believed that psychopaths lack emotions and empathy, but it's more that they don't consider what will happen eventually. It all makes sense when the number of criminals who display these tendencies. Still, another research project found that fully functioning, successful adults with high-flying careers also show the same brain activity as a psychopath.

Here are some signs you can detect a psychopath:

· Superficial charm to lure people in at first

· Ignoring huge problems with a non-committal attitude

· An inflated sense of self

· A need for stimulation from extreme activities

· Lying, conning, manipulating

· Lack of guilt even when pain is caused.

· Shallow feelings, no depth of emotions

· No empathy

· Lacking control, promiscuous behavior, other behavioral issues

· Impulsive, irresponsible, no long-term goals

· A tendency towards criminal activity

The earlier these tendencies are spotted, the more chance you can help someone or even yourself. By letting these traits continue, you are letting it get worse. Psychopaths will use weaknesses against every victim to get what they want. The right thing to do is to extract yourself from the situation, if possible, before you get harmed. If this isn't possible, you need medical help for your loved one.

Narcopath

A narcopath is a narcissist-sociopath mix and is considered the worst type. Someone with an inflated sense of how important they are, as well as a constant need for praise and admiration – which already sounds exhausting! Relationships with them can be addictive but draining as the person with a narcopath will never win.

Here is an excellent checklist for identifying whether you are involved with a narcopath:

· Things move fast – really fast! Instead of getting to know you, a narcopath will immediately make you feel like you've found your soul mate.

· The compliments – at first, they might feel nice, but after a while, you might realize that they're generic and maybe a bit staged.

· Flattery comes in the form of comparisons. It is horrible if it links to an ex. Even if you come out on top, that won't last.

· You have strong chemistry. The passion is off the charts, but not much else is good.

· Hollow eyes that lead to nothing. It's all an act.

· The conversation constantly swivels back to themselves.

· A checkered relationship history is a sign of things to come.

· The silent treatment is standard.

It is another severe form of narcissism that can lead to abuse and violence if left untreated. Some therapy, primarily cognitive behavioral therapy, can help with this.

The red flags of manipulation include:

· Your words being used against you

· They offer you help, but their support leaves you confused and unhappy

· They say shocking things, then claim you misunderstood them

· A lot of what they do is designed to make you feel guilt and shame

· You question your sanity

· Love and affection are withdrawn once you don't obey them

· You fear losing that person, no matter what they do

· You always feel like you fall short of expectations

· You have been on eggshells with that person

· You feel isolated by them

If you feel any of these things happening in your life, you need to start thinking about taking some serious action. Read on for ways to help yourself and the narcissism sufferer.

It's seen as so beneficial that we even have some tips to help you gain some narcissism in your life to boost confidence when times are tough:

· Establish your own identity and don't worry about what others expect of you

· Feel proud when you reach your goals

· Give yourself affirmations

· Consider what you like about yourself

· Care for yourself

· Allow yourself to have imperfections

· When you feel bad, please do something to change it

· Share in the success of others

Chapter 4:
Falling in Love with a Narcissist

There are a lot of people who feel as if narcissists are drawn to them like magnets. It may not be that narcissists are more drawn to you, but you may be willing to hold onto them. When you see certain things, you may not recognize them as narcissistic traits, but they are still unfavorable. Since these are negative traits, most people will not go any further with the relationship.

People are often disturbed by the types of behaviors displayed by the narcissist. They will disengage from the situation because it is easier than dealing with someone problematic from the very beginning. The people who tend to stick around the narcissist will handle this type of situation in a very different way.

If you are a person who feels like narcissists are constantly drawn to you, take a look at your standards for relationships and what behaviors you will and will not tolerate.

To understand whether your standards are healthy and keep you protected, ask yourself the following questions.

- At any point in time, have you ended a relationship because of selfishness on your partner's behalf?
- Are you able to set clear boundaries and stick to them?

- Do you know what behaviors in a relationship you will tolerate and which ones are unacceptable?
- Do you rationalize staying in a bad relationship because you believe it can get better? Is this because of the way things started in your relationship?
- Do you allow your partners to devalue you?
- Is making excuses for your partner's bad behavior commonplace?
- Have you put up with mental, physical, or emotional abuse without leaving?

If you find that these questions relate to you, it is time to sit back and look over your standards. You need to find strategies to help weed out people with destructive behaviors before they sink their claws into you.

Exiting a relationship because you feel that someone is taking advantage of you or having a nefarious intent is not wrong. It may seem challenging to weed out the narcissists, but you simply give them more time to manipulate and take advantage of you when you give people too many chances.

There are also a few different personality traits that narcissists will pick up on and try to take advantage of. Specific characteristics are found to be more helpful to narcissists than others. If you are incredibly empathetic, have a desire to help others, are willing to try harder than most to make relationships work, or your sense of responsibility is strong, you are likely the perfect target for a narcissist.

All of these traits fall into the desires of a narcissist. They will do everything they can to take advantage of your kindness, compassion, and empathy. Most people don't try and hide the positive attributes they hold. Unfortunately, the narcissist can pick his target quite easily.

Narcissists also genuinely enjoy taking advantage of brilliant people. Everything in their lives is a game and roping, someone into their game who is smart feels like a significant win for the narcissist. The high they get from besting an intelligent person is better than many others.

Why are People so Attracted to Narcissists?

If it's true that narcissists are living in constant existential terror (whether consciously or not), why are people so attracted to them? Gradually, cracks begin to appear in the narcissist's idealization of you. He begins to realize that you are not a perfect being. This makes the narcissist feel insecure like maybe the floor could collapse. The narcissist feels betrayed by your failure to remain perfect. He may even become angry with you and start to criticize any tiny imperfection. The narcissist is projecting his insecurities onto you, filling you up with his bad feelings. You were once perfect, but now you are no good. The narcissist must distance himself. All the while, you are trying to understand what went wrong.

As this process unfolds, you start to become desperate to regain the good feelings you associate with being idealized. You become caught in the narcissist's gravity. The narcissist gazes longingly in the mirror, while you gaze longingly at the narcissist.

At the beginning of a romantic relationship with a narcissist, part of the scheme is that Mark will make Claire feel like she has found a regular Prince Charming. He will be everything for her and shower her with love and affection. He will give her everything she needs emotionally, and everything will seem perfect for a while.

This beginning "honeymoon" phase is essentially the hook designed to get Claire craving his constant affection. He will give her everything she wants sexually and be everything she needs in every other respect. Mark will be like a drug, and soon she will become addicted before realizing it. Even the most upstanding, strong, morally conscious, and intelligent people are still human beings with desires. Skilled narcissists will get under your skin and learn your deepest desires. Once this happens, you are at their mercy unless you pick up on the signs early and run as fast as you can!

Unfortunately, Claire does not see any signs of narcissism because she has never met a narcissist trying to manipulate her. She has never surrounded herself with people who were anything other than kind and compassionate, just like her. She loves that Mark has shown his vulnerable side, and he lets her feel like she is helping him through his pain, giving her a sense that she is offering as well as receiving. But over time, this will slowly fade away and reveal itself not to be the case any longer.

After a couple of months, perhaps, things will start to shift, as they always do. The timing will vary based on how the narcissist's plans are proceeding. But soon, the once hedonistic boyfriend is going to turn into something different, but at this point, Claire is madly in love with Mark, and what's worse, she trusts him. He starts to employ those emotional and psychological games which work to tear down her self-esteem and confidence gradually. He will introduce flaws and problems with her friends and family and incite arguments between Claire and those people in her life she loves and values. This will serve to slowly isolate her from those people she once trusted as she leans more and more on Mark, depending on what he tells her because he otherwise gives her what she needs, that is until he doesn't.

These emotional games will gradually tear Claire down until she is just a shadow of her former self. The narcissist may have already employed gaslighting techniques or now begins to introduce them as she focuses on the things that she now perceives are flaws in her character, body, or personality. Now and then, she will get a glimpse of the Mark she knew when they'd first met, and this will keep her going for some time. But it will gradually start to dawn on her that things are not what they seem.

41

One of the first things victims in his situation might pick up on is that the narcissist will become careless about consistency and repetitiveness because they do not care what others think or feel. When she confronts him about this behavior, he will easily deny it and tell her she is making things up—another gaslight symptom. It depends on the victim how far this will go.

Some people have strung along for years and years. Eventually, the narcissist will simply disappear and then reappear sporadically, telling his victim that he is unsure about things and feels insecure about their relationship, perhaps pointing out something that the victim has done wrong that makes him doubt her commitment, etc. The narcissist will use anything and everything at this point to inflict pain and make the victim feel like they need to make up for something they've done.

Eventually, the game is going to end, one way or another. Mark will have gotten bored with Claire and moved on. But frequently, the narcissist will not let go for a very long time, even if they are leaving for long periods between their reappearances. Depending on how strong their chains have become connected to their victims, these victims will simply wait, hope and pray until the next time they see their narcissist partners. The emotional pain and control have run so deep that they do not feel they can live any other way.

When we think of women in physically abusive relationships, many people find it too easy to simply pass judgment on the woman, suggesting that she just needs to leave. She just needs to go. The fact is until you've experienced the kind of emotional abuse and manipulation exercised by an abusive partner, it is impossible to understand just how much a person can twist another human being's reality.

Abuse victims often cite how they simply slipped into a state of denial or were so convinced they were the problem in the relationship that they merely tolerated the abuse and blamed themselves. It is a sad but true reality. Don't ever pass judgment on an abuse victim until you know what you're talking about. And even then, we must all realize that each of us is unique and we all have different constitutions, strengths, and weaknesses. How many times have you heard from someone that they never thought they'd be dumb enough to fall for that, etc.

It's important not to internalize a feeling of being "dumb" if you've fallen victim to narcissistic abuse. The fact is that these people do nothing with their lives except getting better and better at manipulating and hurting others. They are professionals, and they are experts. You are not an idiot for being human and having feelings. You have simply run into someone who knows exactly how to take advantage of your common human decency and kindness.

After the cycle of abuse ends and you've finally gotten free of the narcissist relationship, I hope that you can appreciate that you are lucky to have broken free at all. Many victims have strung along for the rest of their lives to die in misery and isolation without ever having received what they needed and wanted from a romantic partner. A victim going through emotional abuse knows that it is harrowing, and the effects are long-lasting. We now will talk about the emotional upheaval of ending a relationship with a narcissist and the impact of this experience in the long term.

Chapter 5:
Narcissistic Passive-Aggressiveness

W hen we think of passive-aggressive behavior, we often imagine a roommate leaving a sticky note on the bathroom mirror that pretends to be a friendly reminder to put the dishes away. The frustration they feel is thinly veiled. Passive-aggressive people are not aware of how openly aggressive their tactics are.

At some point, we have all been passive-aggressive. You might be trying to let out anger you know is fleeting. Maybe you think what you are doing will solve a problem while avoiding a confrontation. However, for some people, this is the way they navigate social interactions. They will not verbalize what they want. Instead, they leave it up to you to figure it out and then get upset when you don't. They do not dare to come to a person about something bothering them because they think that seems rude.

A passive-aggressive person is much more concerned about not appearing rude than they are about actually being polite. Not wanting to seem harsh is very different from genuinely being concerned about the feelings of others. Instead, their biggest priority is others' perceptions of them. That's why people-pleasing does not come from a selfless place. They will not stand in their truth. They do not know who they are, only that they want to be seen as a good person, and it is essential always to be considered the one in the right.

Emotional manipulators will do favors for you but do not be fooled. These favors come with strings attached. They will be used against you later. They will do things for people and give them gifts only to bring them up later when trying to get you to do something for them. The message will be, "Will you do me this favor? You know, because after all I've done for you, it's the least you could do?" You did not ask for anything. They gave these things to you out of their own free will. That is what makes these gifts nefarious. There was a secret plan, and now if you deny them their request, they say you are a taker and do not give.

The act of being passive-aggressive is a highly manipulative one, whether or not the person using it realizes this. Passive-aggressive people are masters at making it seem like they are leaving the choice up to you when they are secretly leading you towards a specific decision. For example, you are deciding where to go to eat. You suggest a restaurant, and they mumble a very unenthused "okay."

Their tone of voice makes it obvious that they do not want to go to that place at all. You ask them if there's somewhere else they want to go, and they say, "No, let's go there. It's where you want to go." It is highly manipulative because they imply that they will have to suffer through it if you pick the place. This manipulation forces you to let go of the idea, and in desperation for this to be over, you beg them to tell you where they want to eat. Then they say, "Can we go to that restaurant just this once? I usually go wherever you want, but I want to go there this time."

Passive-aggressive people will never say anything productive like, "I'd like to choose where we eat more often. Maybe we could take turns picking from now on?" It would mean that the pain is coming to an end. They expect you to be a mind-reader. You are supposed to know what they want even though they refuse to tell you, and then they get to be angry at you for not figuring it out.

Guilt trips are a favorite tactic among passive-aggressive people. Here is an example of a guilt trip. You have a group project, and on the day your group has agreed to work on it, your friend calls and tells you they have a problem. When you ask them if you can set up a time to talk about it later this evening, they respond with, "Oh, okay. I'll deal with this myself, even though I've listened to you when you needed someone. But it's okay, go work on your project. I know how important it is. I'll be just fine all by myself."

In this situation, even though you told them you would give them what they needed later, it does not keep them from pulling out the shaming tactics. In reality, it is they who won't give an inch, but through playing the victim, they have portrayed you as the unreasonable one who refuses to give anything.

Another of the most popular tactics for passive-aggressive people is the silent treatment. They will not tell you what they are upset about, but they will pointedly let you know that you have done something wrong. It is maddening because while they will not speak to you, they will not leave the room. It causes you to feel highly uncomfortable, which is precisely what they want. They will sometimes even get angry if you try to ask them what's wrong and tell you to leave them alone, but if you do that, you are "walking away" and not fighting for the relationship. You are in a no-win scenario. When they finally tell you all of their gripe, it comes out in a rush. It feels like a tidal wave barreling right at you.

A covert narcissist will often tell you nasty things while expressing emotions of sadness. For example, they will tell you they cannot forgive you for something while at the same time crying. This way, you don't get to be angry at them for what they say to you.

Covert narcissists claim not to be able to express their anger. Ironically, they spend most of their lives angry. Their rage is silent, and it builds up over time. They become bored with the relationship they are currently in, so they start talking to someone else, telling them that all of their partner's shortcomings while conveniently forgetting to mention what they have done wrong. They say this to get sympathy for having put up with such mistreatment.

The cheating has already begun when this happens because they are no longer working with their partner. They spend long hours with another person, speaking badly of their partner, building themselves up as a martyr, while the person they are talking to is saying things like "I'd never do that to you."

Both the narcissist's partner and the person they are speaking ill of are being manipulated because the person outside the relationship is being led to believe they would never be spoken of like this. This is because they are not being given the entire story. They are being told a mere fraction of the truth. The narcissist leads them to believe their partner is the source of all of the relationship problems.

That's why it is so important to be cautious of a person who has nothing good to say about their partner and is talking to you about all the problems in the relationship. It means when they have a conflict with someone, they put all of the blame on the other person and will not take any for themselves. If you are thinking about entering into a relationship with someone like this, there are a few things you need to consider first.

First and foremost, this person makes you feel like there is a chance for the two of you to get together while you are already in a relationship. This means that loyalty is not their strongest suit. They might have you convinced that their partner is the source of all of the relationship problems, but that is one extremely biased account. You have not heard the partner's side of things. If they turn to somewhere outside of their current relationship, they will do the same when the two of you have a problem. Right now, you are bright and shiny because they are love-bombing you and because you haven't spent any real time with them. but make no mistake, you will fall from grace. The question is not if it will happen, but when.

Right now, their partner is the problem. All of their anger and hatred is currently directed at them while you are the one bright spot in their life. You are in the honeymoon phase. If you get into a relationship, their partner will no longer be around to be a scapegoat for their misery. This means that the job will be relocated to you. A narcissist must have someone to place the blame on for their unhappiness. They will not recognize their role in it if they are not satisfied with their life. Something is missing within themselves, but they assume it is because of something the people in their life, especially their romantic partner, are failing to provide for them.

Think about a child who constantly wants a new toy. They have an entire collection of toys that they have not played with for months, and they are poorly taken care of. They think the source of their unhappiness is that they do not have the latest stuffed animal they have their eyes on. They feel like something is missing that will be satiated once they get that particular toy. They genuinely believe they will somehow treat this toy better than the others once they have it because it is unique.

This behavior is expected out of a child, but over time they should learn to value their things better than that. Better loyalty should be instilled into them. Narcissist never grow out of this juvenile way of thinking. The only thing they grow out of is playing with toys. When they get older, they will apply that same mentality to friendships and relationships. The person they are currently dating will no longer be exciting, and they will want someone new.

Chapter 6:
Living with a Narcissist? Do and Don'ts you Should Know About

Working with a narcissist or interacting with one during social gatherings is one thing, but if you live with a narcissist, several instances could lead to friction. Research says that living with a narcissist can lead to toxic relationships; that is true if the narcissist is suffering from very high degrees of NPD and is beyond all help. However, if you are careful about some of the things you do or do not do while living with a narcissist, you can avoid much of the relationship's friction.

The Dos and Don'ts of Living with a Narcissist

• Praise the narcissist from time to time: Narcissists thrive on appreciation. The one thing that keeps them going is praise and approval from others. Humor your narcissist partner from time to time and praise him. This is also true for a woman. This might seem at first that you are only enabling the narcissist behavior, but actually, you are not. Praising him will make him feel you notice him, and chances are that a covert narcissist will also attempt to notify you, even if the circumstances are slim. Yet, it is better than nothing and can establish a relationship of quid pro quo.

• Set clear boundaries: We have spoken about this before. As soon as you start living with a narcissist, be clear about your requirements. Tell him that he can have anything around the house as he wants it to be, as long as you get to have some things as well. The same goes for other areas of your life. Sticking to these parameters and setting boundaries from the very beginning provides a foundation for a stable pattern later.

• Expect them to push back: As soon as you set your boundaries or become assertive, expect them to move around and encroach on your personal space. Narcissists have a hard time dealing with the fact that you have a life of your own or one that does not involve them. So they will put up significant resistance to ensure that you do not always get the things you want or will most likely throw tantrums like a child to get your attention. Stick to your guns, and once they see how strong you are, they will be forced to adjust to your point of view, even if only a little.

• Find a support system: A support group should comprise people you would stand with you through thick and thin. They could be your parents, your best friend, or a colleague at work. If you do not have anyone because you are far from your people, you can always join a therapy or counseling group. The point is to have an outlet where you get a chance to speak for yourself and vent your frustrations without being judged. The narcissist partner at home will have little time or regard for what you have to say, so make sure others are around you.

• Insist on concrete results: When you start living with a narcissist, you will find many occasions when the narcissist promises you this and that, but then you'll notice they never come through. This is one of the many aspects of narcissism; manipulating people and making empty promises to convince the other person to get what they want is a pervasive trait. Put a stop to this as soon as possible and insist on immediate action.

• Expect other kinds of disturbances: A person with NPD is prone to different types of problems. They could be into substance abuse, or there could be similar problems. A narcissist will need professional help and therapy at some point in time, and that is beyond your power.

• Be open about receiving help yourself: Not just your partner, but you should also be mindful and open to the idea of receiving professional service when the time comes. Do not hide your frustrations under the garb of "I am fine" because you are not. The more you acknowledge your predicament, the better you will be able to deal with it.

• No matter what, it only makes sense to focus on the bright side from time to time to make coping easier. A covert narcissist is not always a wrong person; there might be other traits in him that are genuinely good, and he might be good at other things. Focus on them and see how it can enhance both your lives so that co-habiting becomes easier.

• When you decide to live with a narcissist, it is mainly because you might have seen some good in him or he or she has attracted you in some ways. When you do confront the more complex and dark side of a narcissist's personality, it might come as a rude shock to you but do not be in a state of denial about it. Do not try to overlook his possessiveness seeing it as genuine care or his controlling nature as looking out for you.

• Do not internalize what the narcissist says. A narcissist will chastise you in front of others, and they may make remarks about how you are nothing without them at your side. This is designed to make you feel bad about yourself and learn more about the narcissist, which is just what the narcissist wants to satisfy his ego.

• When you live with a narcissist, they automatically assume that you are there because of him, and you should devote your time to him alone. While giving him some attention from time to time is essential, do not make yourself too available. Do not be at his beck and call. Even if you are in the house and the narcissist wants you to do something, tell him you are busy with something else and you will get it done in due time. Chances are, whatever he was asking you to do was for his satisfaction. Do not make it a habit to become the source of his gratification every single time. Distancing yourself from time to time from the very beginning will prevent the formation of a toxic pattern later.

• Do not give in easily: Resist the narcissist from time to time and do not always give in easily to whatever he says. It might seem tempting because giving in to the narcissist's wishes is the easiest way to avoid friction. However, if you make that a pattern, you will be in danger of losing all sense of self. You have to understand that if you make it a habit to give in to whatever he asks, you will completely deprive yourself of everything that is rightfully yours.

• Do not lose yourself: Do not lose yourself when you are in a relationship with a narcissist. Living with a narcissist involves giving him a lot of attention. Do that from time to time because that is what he needs, but do not lose yourself in the process. Take those opportunities to get to shine yourself; dress up every once in a while and revel in the praises people shower on you.

• Do not try to put the narcissist in their place: This can be very tempting, and it is also the only natural to give them a taste of their own medicine from time to time. However, expect a severe backlash from the narcissist when you do that. They are not used to rejection and cannot stand being reprimanded for anything - because they can do no wrong. Trying to put them in their place could lead to volatile situations, so do not engage them aggressively. Being firm but also patient is the best approach with narcissists.

• Do not expect empathy: The sooner you come to terms with this, the better for you. Narcissists are not capable of empathy. A covert narcissist will try because they are usually less aggressive than their overt counterpart, but empathy is something that people with NPD are not capable of. Hence, they will not feel bad for you. Some might articulate that they do, but it is not going to be heartfelt. You need to judge for yourself how much of this you can take and for how long. Make sure you have people around you who will empathize with you in the difficult times when the narcissist does not.

• Do not be afraid to think of alternatives: It is alright if you feel that you want to stay with your partner even if he is a narcissist. However, give considerable thought to your alternatives should you choose to leave. Please do not start thinking that your lives are inextricably linked, and never let yourself believe that you are nothing without him.

Research shows that narcissists are incapable of forming bonds, so they hardly have long-term relationships. Sooner or later, their partners tend to leave, and you could be one of them.

The alternatives could be anything: you could move to a new neighborhood or a new city if you happen to get a new job. You could go back to the things you loved the most but never had the time to indulge in because almost all your time was devoted to your narcissist partner. You could think of dating again when you are ready and accept that not everyone is a narcissist.

Chapter 7:
The Language of Narcissists

T he narcissist can seem unfathomable to the uninitiated. They are adept at manipulation, both emotional and otherwise such that most of their targets do not realize they are being manipulated. Indeed, the narcissist can be construed as an animal a little different from the rest of us. From their motivation to control how they are they perceived or see themselves, they are wired a little differently.

We can thus speak the language of narcissists. When one understands what motivates the narcissist and how they perceive others, one can understand how to protect themselves against them and begin the healing process. Not all narcissists are the same, so understanding narcissists' language starts with learning about the different types.

Men and women with narcissistic personality disorder all have the same essential characteristics - vanity, superiority, entitlement, a lack of empathy, bullying and belittling, and others - but how they manifest can differ. Indeed, the reader will discover that although all narcissists can manipulate and be abusive, others can be worse. This goes without saying. The narcissist may be the type who can engages in a long-term relationship, even if that relationship is fraught with misery for their partner. Or the narcissist can be the type that is so destructive and vindictive that they create a path of destruction all around them in a relatively short period.

Types of Narcissists

The narcissist partner may readily appreciate the traits that help make the diagnosis of the personality disorder. Still, by exploring further the manifestations of this condition, a more robust defense against them can be maintained.

There are many different ways of categorizing narcissism. The primary division in narcissism is between those whose vanity and superiority stem from external characteristics versus those who have grandiosity based on something internal. But as we will see, narcissism can also be categorized based on other factors. It is even possible for a narcissist to have features from more than one type of narcissist.

The narcissist is a strange bird, though the person may not know it. Their vanity and superiority seem natural, and it is normal and natural for them to act based on these characteristics. This is true of all of the different types of narcissism. The following is a list of the major types:

- Somatic narcissism

- Cerebral Narcissism

- Overt Narcissism

- Covert Narcissism

- Seductive Narcissism

- Vindictive Narcissism

- Somatic Narcissism

We tend to think of narcissists as vain based on their appearance, but this is not true of all of them. Indeed, shoving the narcissist into this superficial box allows most to go unnoticed, poising them to wreak havoc on their loved ones and the others around them. The narcissist can have delusions and a sense of superiority based on an external factor, or they can be vain about something that others cannot see, like their intelligence.

The somatic narcissist is the type that is overly concerned with their appearance and sees this as a source of superiority over others. It does not have to be the case that the narcissist actually is better-looking or more fortunate somehow than others; they only have to perceive that they are. It is easy to stereotype everyone who is vain about their appearance as a narcissist. Still, the somatic narcissist engages in the other behaviors and has different thought processes associated with this personality disorder, such as entitlement, and being belittling and demeaning, a need for admiration from others, envy, and lack of empathy.

Cerebral Narcissism

The cerebral narcissist can easily fall under the radar. We do not often think of narcissists as vain or superior about their intelligence, sense of humor, personality, or other qualities about themselves. Still, the cerebral narcissist sees these qualities as the repository of their inflated self. The cerebral narcissist can be a stealthy manipulator and abuser because they do not fit the bill of what most people think a manipulator or abuser looks like.

The cerebral narcissist may not be particularly attractive or prepossessing. We think of the narcissist as obsessed with their appearance—like Narcissus staring at his reflection in the pool—but this type can seem relatively unconcerned with the externals. But they are still narcissists. This type of person may belittle and abuse others based on their perception of a lack of intelligence in the other person. They may be superior in their charm, sense of humor, and great personality. These individuals can be hazardous because they may have internal qualities that attract others to them. These people are just as entitled, envious, and lacking in empathy as the somatic narcissist, charming or not.

Overt Narcissism

Narcissism can be characterized by how explicit the actor is in expressing their qualities to others. Indeed, we can think of narcissistic traits as being those that are more obvious, like bullying and belittling, and those that are more covert, like envy and a need for admiration. The covert narcissist is the bully who is not reticent to demonstrate to others how little they think of them. These are not the seductive charmers who fool everyone; these are the people who place themselves on a pedestal from which they look down upon others - a pedestal that everyone can see.

Covert Narcissism

All narcissists can hide their true selves in order to slither their way into the good graces of others. As a discussion of overt narcissists suggests, if narcissists are honest about who they are, most people would dislike them and be immune to their manipulation. The most effective manipulator and the abuser are the ones who wear an attractive mask, whether it is an external or an internal one. A good manipulator can get you to like and trust them. This is the covert narcissist, the person who acts in secret, perhaps hiding their true nature even from themselves.

Seductive Narcissism

The seductive narcissist does not have to use their body or appearance to gain influence over others. Indeed, the seductive narcissist can be a cerebral narcissist who charms with their winning conversation or great sense of humor. Hot narcissism refers to men and women who wheedle themselves into the confidences of others. This does not have to be a beautiful woman in four-inch heels or a young man with 20-inch biceps and a six-pack. This can be the comedian or the life of the party who is just as effective at seducing women as the men who are more favored phenotypically (if not more so).

Vindictive Narcissism

There is a reason why narcissism is included in the dark triad of perilous disorders. The narcissist is vain and entitled, but he also tend to tear down and destroy them. Some narcissists are more adept at this type of behavior than others. The vindictive narcissist represents the most dangerous subtype of this disorder. We think of vindictive behavior resulting from a slight that sets the other person off. Still, the vengeful narcissist can be triggered by something so minor that it is barely noticeable.

The vindictive narcissist may be inspired to destroy you because you did not attend their birthday party, or you went but were better dressed. Perhaps they noticed their boyfriend spending a little too much time looking at you. The vindictive narcissist desires to destroy you because they are envious of your intelligence, or maybe they just do not like you. What matters is that the vindictive narcissist operates with solid weapons. They will use their words to turn everyone around you against you, even suggesting to others that they should harm you in some way. Vindictive narcissism is more common than people think, and these individuals share a comfortable cell in evil with the Machiavellian and the psychopath.

Manipulation Psychology Used on the Mind of the Victim

We have spoken much about manipulation as the art of the narcissist. We have not delved more deeply into the psychology that the narcissist uses to exert their influence. Narcissists understand human behavior very well, and they know just how to establish power over others. Manipulation psychology is not just about using words to get the target to do this or that; this type of mind control also involves using gestures and being conscious of others' gestures to engage in a kind of suggestive play that most targets are oblivious to.

Recognizing This Type of Mind Control

This type of manipulation is most effective in the beginning of a relationship. Although the narcissist may still have some learning to do as far as reading you is concerned, they will use their manipulation psychology tactics to gain power over you at this stage. The narcissist knows that human beings like to establish rapport with others. Members of our species naturally engage in this sort of dance, so they will use their tricks to develop a rapid and unnatural connection. They will note your subtle gestures, like hand or head movements, and they will copy them.

Though this may seem a silly thing to do, this is a type of suggestion or mind control that causes the other to identify subconsciously with the person copying them. Even ordering the same thing at a restaurant or liking the same things you want, like television shows or movies, is a way of establishing rapport through manipulation. This allows the narcissist to engage in mind control because once they have proved this rapport, you are more vulnerable to suggestion.

It is essential to recognize this type of mind control to break free from the narcissist's hold. Most likely, you have not realized how much information you have given the narcissist. They know your moods and gestures and how to copy them when necessary. And you can easily recognize this type of mind control when you are doing things not in your best interest or when the words of the narcissist make you feel a particular way or seem incongruent with their facial expression (which may be seductive).

Chapter 8:
Narcissist Abuse

A ccording to the Diagnosis Statistics of the NPD, between 0.5% and 1% of the overall population have the disorder, and 50% to 75% are said to men. Mostly narcissism is practiced in learning institutions. Narcissism can be between child-child, adult-adult, or child-adult. Narcissists portray puffed up and irrational traits. These are the same traits used to abuse others. Below are their signs and how they use them against their victims.

Magical thinking: Narcissists use distortion and hallucination known as magical thinking to see themselves as superior and perfect to others.

Entitlement: A narcissist always expects a lot of favorable treatment because they consider themselves unique. Failure to do so they underrates their superiority. They will call you a difficult or awkward person if you fail to comply with them.

Bad boundaries: Narcissists believe that other people exist to meet their needs. There's no boundary between them and others.

Arrogance: A narcissist who feels deflated tries to regain their sense of self-adoration by humiliating, diminishing, and embarrassing someone else.

Shamelessness: They are proud and act shamelessly and never mind about the emotions or wishes of others.

Envy: They envy other people's abilities and may use contempt to depreciate them or their achievements.

Exploitation: Narcissists involve themselves in exploiting others without minding their emotions or interests.

Who is Affected By OCD?

Narcissistic abuse can end in ignoring the behavior, forming relationship triangles, physical abuse, belittling comments, contempt, and sabotage. When there's a fight or an argument between a narcissist and an opposing party, narcissists tend to change the story and present only the parts where the malicious party/person reacted to their narcissism. They later frame it as if that's where the misunderstanding got started.

If they dislike you and intend to bully you, but you happen to defend yourself, they will truncate the story and frame it as you're the bully. They like to spread false information about the person they dislike by gossiping, slandering, and smearing them.

The Sadistic Words of a Narcissist

Narcissists use words to lure their targeted victims. They master very well when, where, and how to strike with their verbal tricks.

They have the forked tongue of both sugar and venom. When the ideal time for full brown abuse comes, they become very generous in throwing poisonous and rotten verbal apples, well-tailored to confuse, belittle, and degrade their prey. Their well-calculated mind games are meant to damage those on the receiving end. They devalue their victims to make them lose their self-worth worth so they can submerge them into their selfish will. Victims are left traumatized, with a great deal of emotional pain. The pain caused seems to be unending; they can become mentally disabled.

Low-Level Abuse

These consist of small, weird comments. In the beginning, they may seem insignificant, but they form the foundation of a narcissist's verbal abuse. This is how they begin to take control of their victims. This often starts early in the relationship. A friendly smile accompanies seemingly insignificant comments; hence, they are rarely recognized for what they are. The victim merely knows that this hidden abuse will advance and continue throughout the relationship.

The Special Union Myth

This is also done mainly at the beginning of a relationship. It is done to convince the victim that they have a special and unique type of companionship.

They may use phrases such as "I have never met a special person like you before." This forms the platform for the victims to feel obliged to tolerate future harmful abuse. They are groomed into thinking that what is between them and the narcissist is exceptional and beyond the ordinary.

The victims are conned into buying into the deceptive idea that the best relationships are explosive and passionate. In these delusions, they never see the signs of abuse trickling in. Even when things fall into a dead-end, they encourage themselves to remain the unique element in their union. With every passing day, they find it very difficult to break things off.

The "I Didn't Mean It" Tease

At this point, the narcissist constantly dismisses insults or criticisms, claiming that they didn't mean what they said. They know very well that the initial comment wounds their prey but makes up excuses to conceal their malicious intention. In reality, this is their way of tactically going on the offensive to put themselves permanently into a dominant position.

False Compliments

Charming and complimentary phrases are the essence of another skill that most narcissists have mastered well. They can praise other people when it suits them, but not a single word is heartfelt. The false praise is to manipulate others, get them onside, and make the criticisms that follow go unnoticed. They may say things like, "I like your character; you are cool and understanding." In other words, this is a means of softening the blows that will follow.

These compliments may seem harmless to the victim and any onlookers. In a way, they may even seem honest. On the contrary, they are just a package of sugar-coated lies. The narcissists themselves don't believe in what they are saying, but it serves their purpose well. It is meant to bait their target.

Projection

A narcissist is never ready to come to terms with reality. Acknowledging their fails, dysfunctional behavior, and malicious intentions are something they are never willing to do. Anything short of perfection is not something they wish to see in themselves. To achieve this, all their faults are projected onto their victim to shift the blame.

Tone Changing

Narcissists can manipulate language with different techniques to get their way. Narcissists employ the most powerful use of language to pursue a silent approach and reach the end goal of the course. During a confrontation, they may choose to glare, frown, shake their heads, turn away, speak softly, or raise their voices. They alter the volume of their voices to convey different messages.

A narcissist applies whatever approach to language is appropriate in their mind. Their words are packaged with venom to poison and bring down the other person. Their intentions are evident to them, but they may demonstrate a different perspective to others. All this is carefully calculated to lure the victim to fall under their control.

How Narcissist Traits can be Harmful

The word "narcissism" is sometimes taken lightly. A better understanding of the term is important. There are some less harmful traits of a narcissist, but these do not matter much. But some of their extreme misdeeds can be toxic to other, and this one matters a lot. These toxic traits are the ones they use to lure, manipulate, and abuse their victims. Let's unpack these harmful behaviors.

1. An exaggerated sense of self-importance

We realize that arrogant people when they need to overstate themselves try to cover up their fragility. The irony is that their need to be recognized as superior has no tangible achievements to back it up. They do nothing to deserve the kind of respect they demand. They look down on others to feel more important. This kind of behavior can be harmful to the people around them.

2. Preoccupation with fantasies

They are preoccupied with always thinking about themselves. The narcissist has an altitude that it is all about them, and others only matter as much as they are helping them achieve their selfish needs. They live in a distorted world where they fantasize about being the undisputed hero. They believe they are above everyone. If you try to outshine them, they will take you down, notch by notch, until you are under their feet. This can mean being harmful to those they strive to take down.

3. Special and unique

In their fantasies, the narcissist believes he is of a higher class. They see themselves as too big to fit into the ordinary slots. They think they can only associate with people on the top of the ladder of success. People with narcissism believe that other people should be regarded according to what they do and not what they are. They do not assign value to the connections they have with their friends. They do not consider values and personal characteristics.

4. An insatiable need for admiration

For a narcissist, the need for admiration can never find satisfaction. They are empty emotional vessels with a hole at the bottom. You eventually run dry and mercilessly yearning for more.

5. Extreme sense of entitlement

Narcissists think highly of themselves, and they expect other people to treat them the same. They believe their expectations should be met without hindrance. The entitlement of the narcissist is hard to live with because it leaves out anyone else's needs. The narcissist's needs always come first. They feel they deserve the royal treatment, and if you are compliant, they will take you down, make nasty comments about you, try to hurt you, and withhold your rights. This is a relationship that can lead to severe depression.

6. Being exploitive

Narcissists take advantage of others to achieve their ends. The narcissist is never afraid of taking advantage of others to satisfy their intentions.

7. Lack of empathy for others

The narcissist is always unwilling to pretend to identify with the feelings and needs of others. They will do a false show of compassion, but it is impossible to sustain because it is just meant to achieve their purpose. As soon as the other party seems not to be cooperating, the true self of narcissist blossoms. Narcissists are not able to tune into other people's feelings. They direct every conversation back to themselves. They ruthlessly turn against the other party.

8. Envious of others and anticipating that others are envious of them

Since narcissists live in an imaginary world where they are undisputed heroes, they believe they are highly admired. They imagine that other people are jealous of their entitlements. They claim that others are envious of them. Their ego gets threatened by anyone who has the potential to outshine them. In the projection of their envy onto others, they do nasty things to bring down their anticipated competitors.

9. Arrogant behaviors

This is a cover-up for their fragility and low self-esteem. It looks like narcissists have a high self-love, but in a real sense, they may be self-loathing. They take others down to feel better about themselves. They make others pay the price of their feeling of vulnerability, self-pity, and anxiety.

This trait is typica of people who have no apologies. Their arrogant nature makes them never acknowledge that they are be wrong. Even when they know very well that they are the one who messed up, they try their best to ensure that someone else carries the blame.

Chapter 9:
Gaslighting

G aslighting refers to a type of psychological abuse used by narcissists to infuse in their victims an extreme sense of confusion and anxiety to the extent that they no longer trust their perceptions, memory, and judgments.

Gaslighting techniques used by narcissists are similar to those used in interrogation, torture, and brainwashing. These techniques have been predominately used in psychological warfare by law enforcement agents, intelligence operatives and covert agencies for decades. It is intended to systematically target the victim's mental stability, self-esteem, and self-confidence to disallow them from functioning independently.

When a victim is being gaslighted, the abuser systematically withholds factual information and replaces it with false and misleading information.

Gaslighting is a subtle manipulative tactic. Thus, it is difficult to detect, and with time, it completely undermines the victim's psychological stability. It is a hazardous form of abuse because it results in significant damages (victims lose the sense of themselves).

When they've been gaslighted over some time, they lose trust in their judgments and even degenerate to the point of questioning the very essence of life. They not only don't second guess themselves, but they also become highly insecure when it comes to decision making.

Furthermore, these victims fall into depression and become withdrawn, making them dependent on their abuser for their sense of purpose and reality. Gaslighting takes away the victim's identity and purpose and replaces it with self-doubt and emptiness.

Gaslighting in Relationships

The people that use gaslighting the most are abusive partners in relationships. A narcissist in an abusive relationship will try to convince the whole world that it is love and intimacy, but the truth is, it's nothing but manipulation. Gaslighting in itself negates genuine love and affection.

Narcissistic relationships follow a pattern, and when it gets to the stage where the abuser begins to show his true colors, he will start to dish out his gaslighting techniques. For example, let's say you and he had plans to go out over the weekend, but when you called to remind him a few days later, he backtracked, saying something like, "I can't remember having such discussion with you, are you sure I'm the one?"

It looks like an innocent response, and at this stage, you won't read too much meaning into it because you're still in a state of bewilderment. Perhaps it might look like you remembered wrong or misheard. When something like this happens in isolation, it might not be gaslighting; it could be that you genuinely forgot, or there was a mix up somewhere. However, when it becomes a consistent occurrence, then questions need to be asked.

As time goes on, you'll start to notice more inconsistencies between the things the narcissist abuser say at different times. For example, you may suggest the idea of visiting a spa for a massage because in the past, he loved going to the hotel. But this time, he might say something like, "I hate going to the spa. Let's go to the beach instead."

Now, it gets a little bit confusing, and you begin to doubt yourself. Was it someone else who said they like spas? Or has the story changed? Suppose you're convinced that they made the earlier statement and are now saying something else. In that case, this might be their way of suppressing and manipulating you into believing that you're not attentive enough.

When the gaslighting moves up to the next level, the abuser will now begin to insinuate that you are the one who is now backtracking from your earlier assertions. How the narcissistic abuser presents the matter depends on the stage of the relationship, but this is an example of such conversation:

Victim: I just informed my mom and dad that you're attending our Christmas dinner. They can't wait to see you.

Abuser: Hey, but we agreed that we need to take some time before we involve family, didn't we?

Victim: But we had this discussion some days ago, and you said you were more than happy to attend

Abuser: I would love to meet your parents, but I told you that we should give it some time. You even agreed. However, the deed is done, and I won't disappoint your parents, so I'll attend.

If you study the conversation above, you'll realize that by agreeing to attend, the abuser is acting friendly and accommodating. As the gaslighting progress, the abuser will continue to explore new methods. From dishing out lies as a response to your statements and questions, they'll begin conversations with lies concerning things done in the past. For example, they'll say something like," You told me I could borrow your credit card, right? Well, I have just bought some items online. I'll make a refund next week.

This time, they cooked up a conversation that shows that you permitted them to spend your money. However, you're convinced that you never did, and they know you didn't, but if you decide to talk about it, they'll concoct more lies and ultimately cloud your mind with some believable stories. Again, this is just a way of increasing your self-doubt in order for them to assume control over your possessions, feelings, and life.

Finally, when the abuser starts to notice that your resolve is getting weaker and weaker, they'll substitute covert deception for straightforward lies. Thus, they will lie about things they/you did or didn't do and things they/you said or didn't say. For example, let's say you started heating water for coffee and had to leave to take care of something else. But when you returned, you saw that they'd used the water for the same purpose. They'll insist, "I heated the water a few minutes ago, but if you say you did, then it's obvious you imagine things. Perhaps you want coffee because you saw me having it."

This might sound funny, but it works like magic, and as time goes on, the victim's self-belief is depleted gradually, until the final stage where it dies.

Gaslighting at Work

Gaslighting knows no bounds, and you can find yourself being gaslighted at your workplace, either by your boss or a co-worker. Most times, perpetrators use it as a tactic to gain or maintain power, but that's not to say that it can't drive the victim crazy. For example, you were given a particular task, and you'd put in so much of your time; however, when you approached your boss, his response was, "But I told you to X instead, why did you waste your time doing this?

Considering the amount of time you've put into the work and the fact that you're sure you did what you were asked to do, you might get a little agitated and even try to be on the defensive. However, you might get a typical response like, "Are you sure you're not over-reacting?"

Or let's say your boss promises to give you a raise if certain conditions are met, and as a dedicated worker, you even exceed those conditions. However, when you bring the matter to his notice, he responds, "I did not promise to give you a raise. I only said I might consider giving you a raise if you met certain conditions, and so far, you've not met any."

Let's say you have a co-worker jostling to get promoted ahead of you and decides to gaslight you. From time to time, you'll realize that they'll say certain things specifically meant to undermine your self-confidence and even make you doubt your worthiness. For example, "Someone said that the director isn't impressed with the report you submitted. Trouble is looming." "Weren't you selected to join the team? Well, I figure you're not good enough to join." "Why are you mad at me? I only said you need to improve your skills."

Gaslighting from abusers isn't limited to words; sometimes, it comes with actions too. For example, you've spent most of your day working on a file on your computer. So, you decide to step out to get some air, but when you get back, you realize that the project has been mildly edited; however, you're confused because you're not sure whether you did it yourself.

Gaslighting is all about perpetuating confusion and insecurities in the victims' lives, and there are a plethora of ways to go about it.

Gaslighting in the Family

As explained, gaslighting describes a deadly form of psychological abuse. The methods used are subtle. Thus, victims are always unaware, and the end product is the distortion of their self-belief and self-confidence. Gaslighting is used by people of different origin, race, religions and even ethnic affiliations. It is also used by friends, lovers, co-workers, bosses, students and family members.

In the family setting, some narcissistic parents use gaslighting techniques to manipulate their children, which destroys their mental development. When children are manipulated into believing that their instincts are wrong all the time, they learn not to trust themselves. Narcissistic parents groom their children to lack any sort of belief in their sense of reality.

It is sad when you think of the thousands of children who depend on their narcissistic parents for teachings and support, only to poison and hinder their development and reality. They constantly seek validation and approval from other people because their instincts and individual voices were silenced years ago.

Whenever they think about themselves, rather than having feelings of internal strength and a strong sense of self, it always results in internal criticism and belittlement. The internal criticism results from the abuse they had suffered at the hands of their narcissistic parent as kids. Even when they have recurring thoughts, they might see it as "being stupid" or from upset, sad or angry. They may believe they are undeserving of these emotions or even "overreacting."

They have been gaslighted to believe they're always wrong. Thus they doubt their very own perception of the world. The saddest part of the situation is that they see nothing wrong in handling things and their entire thought process. They cannot differentiate their genuine thoughts from their projected ways of reasoning.

Chapter 10:
Stop the Narcissism

D ealing with a narcissist is incredibly difficult in the best of times, but there are many different ways to manage your relationship. Regardless of whether you are interested in severing all ties for good or are in a position to continue some degree of contact with a narcissist, understanding some of the ways to deal with the narcissist's toxic behaviors can help you minimize your risks of harm and abuse. You can also cause the narcissist to lose interest in you and move on to other targets when you prove yourself invulnerable to his manipulative tactics.

Consider each method carefully to decide if it meets your needs and helps you, and once you have chosen a strategy, remember to keep it up. No matter how much the narcissist may push and try to get your attention back, be consistent and get the best effect from your actions. None of these methods is easy, and each will take a tremendous amount of effort. Still, when you finally make it to the other side and realize how very free you are from the narcissist's abuse, you will recognize that it was worth every ounce of effort you put into it.

Cutting off the Narcissist

The easiest way to avoid harm from a narcissist is to end the relationship entirely. Refuse to engage in the relationship at all costs. Taking a huge step back from the relationship may be necessary so you can clear your head and see things for what they are. This is typically a permanent change and the only surefire way to ensure that the narcissistic abuse stops. If you refuse to play the game, the narcissist cannot manipulate you.

Furthermore, by refusing any engagement or communication with the narcissist, you can deny the narcissist's strongest motivator: your attention. You suddenly remove yourself as a reliable source of narcissistic supply, and if you continue to deny the narcissist, ultimately, he will have to go elsewhere to meet his need.

Keep in mind that when you do this, there will be a period called an extinction burst by psychologists. Consider an experiment in which a rat is taught to press a button to get a tiny nibble of candy. The rat very quickly learns to expect that candy every time the button is pressed, and the behavior of pressing a button becomes positively reinforced. The rat does this to get the sweet and does so repeatedly. If the rat goes up and presses the button and one day, it just stops giving out candy, and the rat will be confused. It will encourage the button repeatedly, with increasing enthusiasm, as it desperately tries to force it to do what was expected and provide more candy. Over time, the rat will lose interest when it becomes clear there is no further reaction, but it will go back to the button occasionally and try to press the button.

Take a Break from the Relationship

Similar to cutting off the narcissist, taking a break from the relationship involves a refusal to communicate. In this case, however, it is not permanent. The suspension is intended to allow you to clear your head and reevaluate whether you want to continue. Regardless of what he may accuse you of, remind yourself that this is not a punishment. You did not make this decision to hurt him; you made it protect and care for yourself. You are entitled to controlling who you communicate with, and if you decide that you do not want to talk to the narcissist, you are within your rights to make that choice.

When taking a break, it is appropriate to tell the person and to discuss things when you are ready. You do not have to provide him with a timeline, no matter how much he may bug you for one, and at that point, you can refuse all future contact. You are giving yourself the chance to cool off. Ensure that you do not say something that will make the situation worse or inflame the narcissist into doing something harmful.

Do not let the narcissist goad you into accusations of abuse or playing the victim. You are making a choice that works for you, and ultimately that is the essential part. You need the breathing room, and you are taking it. Remind yourself that you owe it to yourself to care for yourself, especially when no one else will. You cannot care for others if you are not caring for yourself.

Healthy Boundaries

Sometimes, cutting off a narcissist is not a viable option, and that is okay. When you have no choice but to continue contact, such as if bound by a court order to continue a co-parenting relationship, or you work with the narcissist and are not in a position to leave your job, you can focus on mitigating as much harm as possible and protecting yourself from the toxicity the narcissist seems to exude naturally.

Healthy boundaries are the most straightforward techniques to minimize harm from a narcissist, but they are difficult. These boundaries represent a line between what is acceptable and unacceptable, and they are to be set at your prerogative.

When the narcissist challenges a boundary, give him one warning. Tell him that if he continues to test your limits, you will provide a consequence. Tell the narcissist what that consequence for stomping on your boundary is, and every time it is done, you need to enforce the result. If you tell the narcissist that you will take an extended break if your boundary is broken, follow through on it. If you tell him you will stop talking if he calls you names in anger, you must immediately disengage and walk away. The key here is to follow through with the natural consequence, no matter how much the narcissist may cry, beg, or threaten.

Disengage

Disengaging does not mean ignoring or bottling your feelings, however. When you acknowledge what was said and give it the consideration it deserves, which is, admittedly, very little, this can be particularly difficult if the narcissist is a loved one you trusted, but remember to disregard his emotional reactions to the words that protect you. You do not fall into the narcissist's trap, and you do not let the narcissist regain control over your emotions, and in return, the narcissist will slowly lose interest.

The Grey Rock Method

Similar to disengaging emotionally, the grey rock method involves minimizing emotional reactions, but in this case, it is ignoring all interactions, both good and bad. Aim to avoid as much interaction as possible, and when you are forced to interact, keep it boring and meaningless. The name alludes to a grey rock on the side of the road. Consider how often you notice and remember all of the rocks you walk past in a given day—the answer is most likely none. People do not pay attention to something as mundane and worthless as a grey rock on the side of the road. Your goal in this method is to be as ordinary and useless to the narcissist as the grey rock. If you can achieve this state of mediocrity, the narcissist will slowly lose interest in you.

The trick is to be robotic in your responses. No matter how angry you may feel in response to whatever was said, respond in as few words as possible, and make sure it is never immediately after the message was sent (if it does not warrant an immediate response). For example, imagine that he messaged you saying that you are beautiful and he loves you. This should be ignored. Five minutes later, he messages asking how your shared child is doing. Give him the bare minimum answer while still being comprehensive. List what she is doing, whether she is sick, and maybe what she ate for dinner, but keep the interaction as emotionless as possible. Do not emote, no matter how tempting it may be.

Be Realistic

Keeping your interactions with the narcissist realistic will keep you from setting up high standards that she will never meet. Telling yourself that she will never be emotionally supportive and lacks empathy will help you keep reality in mind when dealing with a narcissist. If you are fully prepared for the narcissist to respond in a typical fashion, you will always be prepared, no matter how she responds, and you may even find that you are surprised upon occasion. This is key when maintaining a relationship with a narcissist, whether romantic, platonic, workplace, familial, or co-parenting. You are protected from the disappointment of narcissistic behavior.

Focus on the Positive

Likewise, when interacting with a narcissist, remembering to focus on the positive helps you recognize things that you enjoy about the person. After all, something must have attracted you to the narcissist at some point, and you may be happy to see tiny semblances of that person in the narcissist in front of you. While the personality is still likely vastly different from the one you met at first, there still may be parts of the narcissist that at least make her tolerable.

For example, she may be horrible at emotional support or anything but being the center of attention. Still, she may also genuinely be a good cook, and she loves to entertain all of your friends, or she may be brilliant. You enjoy the intellectual conversations you have over coffee, even if they involve occasional snide comments about how you do not understand because are not educated. Reminding yourself of the positives helps when you are ready to lose your temper with the narcissist, as outbursts would be detrimental.

Decide Your Hill to Die On

The last vital tactic to remember is to choose your hill to die on wisely. This is a fancy way of saying choose your battles carefully. Though narcissists seek out confrontation-avoidant people on purpose, avoiding conflict can prevent detection. For this reason, you always pick your battles wisely and be prepared to engage in a match only if you genuinely want to deal with the aftermath.

While some things are worthy of a dispute, such as a co-parent choosing to drive with children in the car while drunk, an argument over who said something first is petty, and the narcissist is not likely ever to concede or admit that he is lying. For this reason, only choose battles if you are willing to fight them. If you are unwilling to deal with the aftermath and ultimately do not bother fighting over it, whatever the narcissist did is insignificant.

Chapter 11:
A Hidden Narcissist Suffers Internally?

Narcissists are continuously overlooked for their good characteristics. Yet, they are vulnerable people who need understanding. They create their model through others and require self-identity when isolated. They are usually scared of getting a proper study of their behavior because the consequences would be frightening. Many are spiritually wasted, so they must explore getting support from another person. When describing a narcissist, you will see an egotistic character with an overblown personality. In reality, they depend on others for their thinking and attitudes.

Their thinking is defined by anxiety, uncertainty, and delusions. The unenthusiastic victim leaves them weak, helpless and hurt. They visualize themselves as a higher being, and when it is evident, it is impossible to live with.

Narcissistic behaviors are based on certain mindsets and beliefs that associate power with others' ill-treatment. This belief system makes narcissists view their peers as weak and inferior those do not need any attention. A narcissist person also believes that a person's worth is derived from his superiority or inferiority. These attributes are exhibited through emotions like rage and anger.

The mentality of a narcissist can cause him to detach from the feelings of others. It explains why most narcissists will never connect with the pain and challenges of their peers or relations. It also explains why they will always dismiss their complaints.

In the mind of a narcissist, a partnership does not need to exist in relationships. To him, any relationship must have a top dog and an underdog. The narcissist will continuously fight to be superior or the top dog. The general belief is that human beings can either rule or be ruled. Such a mentality causes narcissists to feel entitled to a certain kind of treatment.

Another mindset assumed by narcissists is that people are only there to serve their needs. They ignore others' needs because they think others do not need comfort and assistance. To them, it is the responsibility of their partners to serve and provide comfort. The narcissist wants to be adored, praised, and valued all the time.

In a nutshell, life with a narcissist is all about competition. Narcissists will compete with their colleagues, family members, and partners to ensure they remain in control. Due to this, narcissists never rest. They stay on the offensive to keep others admiring their courage. Their behavior revolves around building their status and interests.

Here is the thought pattern of a narcissist who is wired differently. Some of the common thoughts that keep running through their mind are:

· 'Why am I not getting the attention I need?'

· I only need to concentrate on myself and take care of my own needs.'

· I need to get out of this relationship because I do not feel in control.

· I am always right, you are always wrong, and you can do nothing about this fact.

· Why do I need to feel bad for someone else?

· I deserve some appreciation. Why have I not received it?

· I feel bored; it's time to stir things up.

· Why do you think you are to cause me shame?

Narcissists will avoid every activity or behavior that make their codependents feel appreciated. Their strategies are fashioned towards tearing others down. For a narcissist, there is the only method of winning – controlling the minds of other people. Sadly, with all the attention and admiration they receive, they rarely get pleased. They only feel suitable for a short while, then get back to doing hurtful things to remain in dominance. That is why most of them stay miserable for a good part of their lives.

Chapter 12:
The Narcissist's Target

N arcissists are emotional predators, and the fact that you're a human makes you automatically vulnerable to their antics. That said, it makes sense to identify the traits that narcissists identify in their targets, especially when you realize that you are being targeted for exploitation.

When you consider these traits, you'll realize how wonderful they are, especially if allowed to blossom in a healthy and loving relationship. Sadly, a narcissist will only use them to manipulate, exploit and damage their victims. Below are some of the traits that narcissists look out for in their potential victims:

1. Conscientiousness

2. Empathy

3. Integrity

4. Resilience

5. A high degree of sentimentality

Conscientiousness

Many people do not realize this, but one of the prime qualities a narcissist seeks is his potential victim's ability to be conscientious. Conscientious people are always concerned about others' wellbeing and carry out their obligations to others. They are vulnerable to narcissists because their decisions are tied to their conscience. Sadly, they project their sense of morality onto the narcissist, assuming he will do the same.

They know that a conscientious person is one of the very few people that would grant them numerous chances, give them the benefit of the doubt, and even care more about them than their personal needs.

Narcissists love to target conscientious people for romantic relationships because they know that moral people see caretaking as an obligation, especially in relationships. They know that these people are ready to fulfil their obligations even if they feel endangered or if it puts them in harm's way.

Empathy

Every narcissist's joy is to encounter an empathic victim because narcissists, in general, do not get a constant narcissistic supply (attention, praise, resources, etc.) from people who lack empathy - like themselves. Thus, the importance of securing a narcissistic target cannot be overemphasized.

Narcissists cannot show empathy towards others, but they carefully target people who have a great deal. The physical and emotional validation that empathic people give narcissists helps maintain their bloated ego and feelings of authority; otherwise, they practically starve and renew their hunt for a new supply source.

When you take everything into consideration, you'll realize that empathic people are the opposite of narcissists, and their attitude helps to empower narcissists in their abuse cycle. For example, the fact that an empath is always willing to see the narcissist's perspective even in the height of abuse maintains the abuse cycle repeatedly. As if that is not enough, narcissists identify with empathic people because they know that they're the ideal audience for their pity ploys even after highly abusive incidents.

If you happen to be an empathic person, understand that narcissists believe they can just put out a faux apology or create a sob story to write off their abuse. They do this because they know you'll always try to see reasons behind their toxic behaviors and even make excuses on their behalf.

They depend on your God-given ability to forgive and sympathize with them, irrespective of the ill-treatments they've subjected you to in the past. Most times, narcissists can escape retribution and accountability for their actions because they appeal to their victims' empathy.

It is tough to pretend to be someone you are not, and as such, empathic people constantly second-guess their decisions to punish narcissists for their actions because they feel an unbearable amount of guilt when they see the narcissist being prosecuted (either by society or law). Thus, they are inclined to protect their abusers instead of exposing them to the world.

Integrity

This might sound very funny, but narcissists are incredibly attracted to people who keep to their words. For example, if it is not a moral code to cheat or give up on a relationship prematurely, who stands to benefit? The narcissist, who is morally and mentally impoverished! While the victims feel morally apprehensive about betraying the relationship, retaliation, or even withdrawing from their supposed obligations to the narcissists, the narcissist in question maintains zero remorse for harming their victims.

The victim possesses a rare gift that benefits them and their partners in a healthy and productive relationship. However, this same gift becomes a weapon in the hands of a narcissist – a deadly weapon used to destroy their self-worth and self-belief.

Resilience

The most painful part about being a victim of narcissistic abuse is realizing that you weren't wrong most times. As a victim of narcissistic abuse, your ability to bounce back from your abuser's cruel acts is something that strengthens your bond with him.

Resilience is an excellent quality to possess, especially when faced with adversities of life. Still, in an abusive relationship, the victim's resilience is exploited and used against him/her to keep them enslaved in the web of deceit and manipulation.

Even though resilient people are more aware of the dangers, they still find it challenging to give up on their abusers even after multiple abuse incidents. Typically, they will choose to disregard their instincts and fight for the relationship, assuming the role of a "fighter" or "savior," as they put in the energy to keep an unsustainable relationship afloat.

The saddest part about the resilient victim is that there are times when they even quantify their love by the amount of abuse they've suffered at the hands of their abuser. Unknown to them, this occurs because they have successfully developed an abusive bond with their toxic and offensive partner.

High Sense of Sentimentality

There is no gainsaying that narcissists are overbearing, petty, and manipulative. Thus, sentimental targets capable of falling deeply in love are incredibly appealing to narcissists because they know they can use love-bombing (extreme praise and flattery to groom a victim) to manipulate them easily. During the early stages of narcissistic relationships, narcissists shower their victims with so much love and attention; the idea is to secure their trust, and in this case, appeal to their craving for love. It is a strategy that works very well! They intentionally create sweet memories they want their victims to romanticize during future periods of abuse.

Narcissists love to play with their victim's emotions; they know they can get their victims hooked before they start to withdraw by creating a fraudulent "soulmate" effect that will cripple their victims and leave them wanting things to be as they were during the early stages of the relationship.

Narcissists find it very easy to trick empathic and sentimental people. The only thing they do is to fraud their victims into believing they're kicking off a meaningful, long-term relationship. Mind you, it is very typical for people to want to maintain long-term, healthy relationships, but it becomes a problem when a predatory narcissist is involved.

Why did the narcissist target you?

You have something the narcissist wants (lifestyle, power, money, position). In a narcissistic relationship, certain things come into play. First of all, it begins with a hook – a dream, most times. You think it is all about you and your wellbeing, by the truth is that the narcissist is all about control.

There are occasions where the narcissist will appear to be helpful, but when things don't go as planned, the tables will turn on you. However, when you realize the pattern and opt to hold him accountable for his actions, things get out of hands and degenerate rapidly.

Chapter 13:
Narcissist and Relationships

Charming You

During the charming phase, the narcissist will set you up as an ideal person that everyone should strive to get to know. Through intense observation, they will figure out just what you desire in a relationship. Then in a brief time, they prove to you that they are all you have been looking for and more. They lay on the charm fast and quick by love-bombing you.

Is there something you've always wanted to do but have never gotten around to? They will make it happen. Is there some need you have that you've always wished could be fulfilled? They're going to take care of it ASAP. At first blush, the narcissist seems to be everything you have ever wanted. But that's not true. They're only assuming a persona that matches all you've sought in a relationship. This persona will be discarded when they feel they've got you to hook, line, and sinker.

Making you feel worthless

The narcissist will make you feel like your life has no meaning. She does this without fail. It's the next thing to expect after she has spent such a short time loving you a little too intensely. Once they've got you believing that they are the one you've waited for your whole life, what happens next? They proceed to yank the rug out from underneath your feet. Next thing you know, this very same person who was full of praise and worship for you will take every chance she can to make you feel like crap. It's a bait and switch situation.

Now you find yourself wondering what happened to the person you got to know at the start of the relationship. Where did they go? They have got to be there somewhere. Perhaps they are only going through a rough patch, so you do anything and everything within your power to regain their approval and love, hoping that a change in your attitude and behavior will be enough to bring them back, so you can continue to enjoy their attention and love.

Hogging the Conversation

Where you used to be the star of the relationship, that changes. The narcissist will supplant you and become the only one worthy of note. All conversation becomes strictly about the narcissist. Otherwise, it's not worth engaging in. For the narcissist, it is delightful to watch your frustration as whatever attention you used to enjoy from him is consistently being taken away, and more importantly, given to him instead. It's a thrilling power move for the narcissist you have the great misfortune of dating.

Violating your Boundaries

The narcissist will be completely aware of things you do not take lightly and decide that those are the exact things she's going to mess with. She will watch as you grow incredibly frustrated with her. She will enjoy the constant emotional rollercoaster you put her through, as she convinces you she never meant to hurt your feelings.

The truth is that the narcissist has been out for blood since day one. She wants to hurt your feelings. This is how she controls you. She wants to watch as the so-called "boundaries" you have set up for yourself are slowly but surely eroded by the sheer force that she is. It's a game, and it's intoxicating for her to watch you become a shadow of yourself.

Breaking the Rules

In line with testing your boundaries and pushing past them, the narcissist will break the rules. They know that certain things are a no-no for you, but they will go right ahead and do stuff they know you disagree with anyway.

You and the narcissist could have a conversation about something they did, and they will agree with you that, yes, they ought never have behaved that way. But guess what happens after a few days or weeks? The narcissist goes right back to doing the same things — but worse. Why does he do this? He knows that constantly breaking the rules is a surefire way to hurt you in the end. He knows that this is the best way to program you to be okay with his games.

Changing You

When you begin dating the narcissist, be careful if your friends and family constantly talk about the fact that you're changing, and not in a good way. The fact that they're able to tell you this is a good thing; it means your narc lover has not yet completed her mission of isolating and walling you off from the people who love you.

Negative Emotions and Feedback

Dating a narc never feels good. It's like you're caught in a tsunami of negative emotions. You have to deal with their insecurities, their manipulative lies, and their general awfulness. At some point, you'll begin to wonder whether or not you're good enough as a human being. This is the natural thing to do because the person who once thought the world of you now feels that you leave much to be desired and aren't doing your best to be better. Whatever that means.

Making Everything Your Fault

In a relationship with a narcissist, you're going to find that you're somehow always causing trouble. That's how devastating the narcissist can be when you are in a relationship with her. At no point is the narcissist going to accept responsibility for whatever it is they have done. All their actions and words are going to be on your shoulders.

If you had not been a certain way or had simply gone along with everything they told you, everything from A to Z would not have happened. I recall my mother once telling me that I was responsible for all the evil in the world. I wanted to ask her how back then, as it made no sense to my innocent, child-like mind. Now I understand that for the narcissist, logic is overrated. It doesn't need to make sense. If they say such and such is like so and so because of you, it simply is.

Chapter 14:
Empathy

A sk yourself the following questions to determine if you're an empath:

• Can you perceive people in some way?

• Do you feel people's emotions and mistake them for yours?

• Can you think along the same line as other people?

• Do your feelings change as soon as you meet a particular person?

• Do you sometimes wonder whether you're co-dependent, neurotic, or even crazy?

• Can you read peoples' minds?

It can be awesome having the ability to pick up on other people's energies. Still, it can be a real struggle on the downside when the said energies are dark, especially if the empath in question knows nothing of their ability.

As an empath, these are some traits that you're bound to display:

Highly Sensitive

People keep on telling you that you're too sensitive. This is because what they say or do affects you easily. You can read into their unsaid messages when they talk or do something. This sensitivity can make you susceptible to things that don't hurt well-adjusted people. Your high sensitivity makes you give a lot of thought to what you do or say. This pattern always leads to self-inhibiting tendencies. You end up customizing yourself too much so that the world can fall in love with you. The habit of suppressing your genuine emotions comes with a cocktail of challenges.

Soak Up Other Peoples' Energies

You could be having a fantastic day with your spirits high, and then you go to Starbucks and sit next to a family who, unbeknownst to you, just lost one of their members. Nothing is said. All are sipping at their coffee with quiet faces. Ever so slowly, the joy you first had begins to fade away, and in its place, sadness takes over. You have no reason to be sad, but you experience this sadness anyway. Soon, the family gets up, troops out of Starbucks, and then your sadness fades away. You had just absorbed their energies.

Introverted

Being introverted is not the same as being shy. A shy person might loathe being alone and feel rejected for a lack of human contact, but on the other hand, an introvert gets drained when they stay too long with other people, and they cherish being alone. A shy person has self-inhibiting tendencies, but an introvert has a strong sense of self and stays true. Empaths are more likely to be introverted than extroverted. They don't shun all human contact but prefer socializing on one-on-one terms or within small groups.

Highly Intuitive

One of the most effective weapons in an empath's hands is their gut feeling. They can sniff out the true nature of a situation. This makes it a bit hard to play games with an empath. They will see right through your tricks. As an empath, if you meet someone, you tend to have a gut feeling of what that person is really like. You are always in tune with your surroundings and can tell when there's danger.

Overwhelmed By Relationships

Conventional relationships spend as much time together as possible. An empath cannot thrive in this kind of arrangement because they constantly pick up on their partner's emotions and mistake them as their own. This is not to say that empaths cannot form any relationships. However, the traditional relationship needs to be deconstructed. For instance, they can have a room of their own that they may retreat to when their urge to be alone kicks in, and also, their partners should be patient with them.

Take Long To Process Emotions

The average person has laser attention on their emotions. Whether sadness or joy, it kicks in suddenly. Their emotional reflexes are fast too. An empath takes the time to understand the feelings they are currently feeling. For instance, if something terrible goes down, the sadness won't register immediately. They will first try to process the situation, going over the details time and again, and then the sadness will accumulate inside. They can experience emotions in such a powerful way. Thus, whether it's sadness or joy, they feel it completely.

Love Nature

Most empaths are at their happiest when surrounded by nature. Whether it's the sunlight kissing their skin, the rain falling on them, or taking in a gulp of fresh air, no other activity restores their balance as much as being surrounded by the natural world. They feel a deep sense of connection with nature. When an empath is experiencing a tsunami of emotions, one of the therapeutic measures would be taking a stroll through an open area beneath the sky.

Strong Senses

An empath boasts of very developed senses. They can catch the slightest whiff of an odor, see into the shadows, hear the tiniest sound, and feel the vibrations of various other things. These developed senses make them really good at noticing the small stuff. Empaths seem to see what would ordinarily escape the attention of most people. For this reason, they tend to flourish in careers that demand close attention and the exploration of the abstract.

Generous

There isn't a more selfless person than an empath. They don't have to have something to help. For instance, when an empath comes across a street child and sees her suffering, it tugs at their heart. They want to give her some food and find a way of removing her from the streets. The majority of the world doesn't care about street children and sees them as an annoyance. We assume that the world's empaths play a critical role in helping street children and other people experiencing hardship.

Creative

Empaths tend to be very creative. This is aided by the wealth of emotions they are constantly experiencing. Their creative nature manifests itself in almost every aspect of their life — food, relationships, homes, and most importantly, one's career. An empath is likely to do well in the arts. They have tremendous potential when it comes to drawing, writing, singing, or making films. They tend to portray their emotions unambiguously and can capture the feelings of other people as intended.

People are Drawn to You

If an empath isn't aware of their unique gift, they are likely to hide from the world. They would rather hide and be safe than stay among people and experience every emotion imaginable. This can make society grow suspicious and even hate them. However, if an empath is self-aware and knows of their ability to soak up the energies floating around them, then people will be drawn to them. People know that empaths have a tremendous capacity to understand and help them get through whatever challenges they are facing.

Empaths Fall into the Following Distinct Categories:

• Geomantic empaths: These empaths are tuned to a particular environment or landscape. Geomantic empaths are connected to specific sites like buildings, lakes, oceans, and mountains. These empaths feel the historical emotions of these sites. For instance, if an empath visits an area where people were slaughtered many years, they can still feel the sorrow. Empaths attach feelings to different environments so that each setting evokes certain emotions. Such empaths tend to carry souvenirs to remind them of various backgrounds.

• Physical empaths: Also known as medical empaths, they pick up on the condition of someone else's body. They instinctively know what ails another person. In extreme cases, they can pick up on the symptoms to share in the other person's pain. Physical empaths also have healing abilities. They tend to take careers in conventional or alternative medicine. Physical empaths are great at taking care of unhealthy people. Those who have ailments trust them instinctively because they feel that they care.

• Emotional empaths: They are sensitive to the emotional energy floating around them. As an emotional empath, you will absorb other people's emotions and think they are yours. This can be deeply distressing if you're constantly around negative people. An emotional empath should increase their self-awareness to distinguish their emotions from those of others. Emotional empaths tend to withdraw from other people so they can spend time alone and recharge. An emotional empath should protect their energy by following various healing practices.

• Animal empaths: You have certainly seen someone in your neighborhood who is more interested in keeping company with animals than humans. They have a specific pet or even various pets that mean the world to them. There's a high likelihood that such a person is an animal empath. An animal empath feels a deep connection with animals. They sense what the animals want, and the animals love them back. The link is so deep that they have a way of communicating with each other. An animal empath answers to their intense desire to connect by domesticating their animals of choice. Also, they tend to be passionate about animal rights and contribute to funds that advance animal welfare.

• Plant empaths: A plant empath shares a deep connection with a particular plant or plants in general. The plant evokes certain emotions when they touch it. A plant empath can communicate with the plant and know its condition. They like hanging out near the plant in a natural environment, bringing it into their house or planting it in the garden.

• Precognitive empaths: Are you the type of person who can always tell the future? And this is not for you alone, but also for unrelated people or events? You're certainly a precognitive empath. You tend to "see" things before they come to pass. Your visions are made manifest in various ways, such as dreams or feelings. Having this ability to foresee the future is both rewarding and distressing. It can help you brace for the future, and at the same time, it can amplify your misery, knowing the pain that awaits.

Chapter 15:
Co-dependency and Narcissists

C odependency and narcissism are two sides to the same coin. They both lack a healthy sense of self and struggle with defining who they are, bringing a whole barrage of issues to the table. Ultimately, codependency and narcissism are two different reactions to similar situations. Whereas the narcissist learns to be overtly selfish, the codependent learns to be overtly selfless. However, they are not always strictly opposites. In some cases, the two can overlap to some degree; someone can exhibit codependent behaviors in certain situations while behaving narcissistically in other contexts. For example, someone could be very codependent in a marriage or relationship, seeking to cater to their spouse's every whim, but be quite narcissistic with other people, such as friends or strangers. Though narcissism and codependence are both quite different, their root cause is the same.

What is Co-dependency?

In many normal relationships, we develop dependent relationships. This means that we prioritize our partners and rely on each other for love and support. The connection is mutually beneficial, and neither person worries about expressing their genuine emotions. In a dependent relationship, both people enjoy time spent away from the relationship while still meeting the other's needs.

However, in a codependent relationship, the codependent feels that his only worth comes from being needed. He will make huge sacrifices, martyring himself to ensure the other person's needs are met. He exists solely for the relationship and feels as though he is worthless outside of that relationship. The association is with his only identity, and he will cling to it at all costs; within that relationship, he will ignore his own needs and wants, feeling they are unimportant.

Causes of Co-dependency

Like NPD, many external factors are believed to cause a codependent personality to develop. This is because both codependency and narcissism are similar personality flaws, stemming from the exact root cause of damaged self-esteem.

Poor Parental Relationships

Frequently, people who have developed a codependent personality have grown up repeatedly having conflicts with their parents throughout their childhood. Their parents may have prioritized themselves or somehow otherwise denied that the child's needs were essential. By constantly downplaying his needs, the child internalizes that those needs are not important. After all, if the child's parents could not be bothered to tend to them, they must not matter.

The child learns to prioritize his or her parents instead and feels greedy or selfish when committing to self-care. Frequently, this kind of relationship between parent and child happens because they have an addiction problem and will do anything to feed the addiction. The parent never matured past the selfish development stage as a child and focuses solely on him or herself. Because of all the time spent focusing on the parent's needs, the child never develops the independence and identity necessary to succeed in life. Feeling incomplete when not needed, these people frequently seek out other enablers that allow them to continue living in this fashion.

Living with Someone Dependent on Care

When a child grows up around someone else who requires regular or around-the-clock care beyond the realm of the normal, whether due to severe illness, injury, or some sort of mental illness, the child's needs go unmet in favor of meeting more pressing ones. The child is pushed aside in favor of the person who needs care, and the child's needs become less essential to internalize. The child may also consider the dependent person who is causing his needs to be put on the back burner as he takes care of someone who literally cannot care of herself.

Living with a family member who requires extra care does not necessarily cause codependency to develop, and many people make it through the caregiving stage without issue. But certain personality types are predisposed to codependent tendencies. It becomes an issue if the young child is dependent on care, and the parent tends to focus entirely on the dependent person instead of spending the time the child needs to grow and thrive.

Abuse

It is no surprise that abuse, whether physical, emotional, or sexual, leaves lasting harm on a child. While some children go on to abuse others, others fall into a pattern of codependency. A child exposed to repeated abuse eventually begins to develop a coping mechanism to suppress her feelings. This leaves her only caring about other people's needs while neglecting her own.

Abuse victims also tend to seek out people with similar tendencies as the abuser as this is what is familiar. They know how to live through the abuse and understand that the relationship will often revolve around codependent behaviors. Abusers and narcissists love codependents, as codependents tolerate vast amounts of abuse that would make other people baulk.

Key Features of Co-dependency

Frequently, codependency manifests itself in incredibly recognizable ways. Though every person is different, and behaviors will change depending on the relationship, there are several patterns associated with codependency. Knowing how to identify these will enable you to recognize when you or someone you know is exhibiting codependent tendencies. If you feel that you may be codependent, seeking a trained psychologist's professional opinion would be a great place to start your journey toward understanding yourself.

· Exaggerated sense of responsibility: Codependents frequently feel as though the weight of their loved one's actions is on their shoulders.

· Confuse love and pity

· Doing more than their fair share

· Sensitive when good deeds are unrecognized: When a codependent feels as though her efforts have gone ignored, she is likely to feel hurt or as she is not good enough. She will try to martyr herself further to get the recognition she craves to soothe her low self-esteem and prove that she matters.

· Feeling guilty when caring for self: Any time the codependent engages in acts she sees as selfish or unnecessary in the grand scheme of things, she will feel guilty. After all, her needs should be met last, and if she does anything other than that, she is behaving selfishly, which is unacceptable.

· Rigid: Codependents do not tolerate change. They often seek out familiar things for this reason, which leads them to constantly seek out other enablers in relationships, even if these enablers prove to be abusive.

· Cannot set healthy boundaries: Codependents see no boundaries between themselves and their enablers. They have no sense of self outside the relationship or apart from the enabler. Because they fail to set boundaries, the relationship eventually consumes their lives and leaves little room for anything else. This lack of limits also leads to needs going unmet.

· Needs recognition to feel whole: Without recognition for their good deeds and caring for others, codependents feel unwanted and unimportant. They require people to recognize their actions to help bolster their fragile self-esteem.

· Need to control others: Codependents, feeling utterly responsible for their enablers' actions, also seek some level of control over their relationships. Because codependents always do everything possible for the enablers, they develop the control they desire, and the enabler allows them to have it. Without power, the codependents feel unable to help.

· Fear of abandonment: With their subpar self-esteem and feeling as though they have no sense of identity beyond their relationships, codependents are terrified of being abandoned.

· Poor decision-making skills: Frequently, their dysfunctional opinion and view of their relationships make codependents opt for bad decisions. These could range from refusing to leave a dangerous situation because they want to stay with their partner or refuse to meet their needs, even if it makes them sick or hurt.

· Difficulty communicating: Codependents struggle to communicate their own needs and wants because they are so caught up in the idea that they do not matter. Even if they hate something, they will refuse to say it if they think it would be detrimental, even slightly, to the other person.

· Unhealthy dependence on relationship: Codependents exist solely for their relationships and enablers, and that dependence crosses the line into the territory of dysfunction.

· Untrusting: Frequently, due to so much dysfunction in childhood, codependents tend to distrust those around them, especially those who insist that their needs be met or they try to point out that their relationship is unhealthy.

· Confrontation-avoidant: Codependents avoid confrontation at all costs. They have developed a tendency to avoid their own needs to avoid confrontation, and that tendency has extended well into adulthood. The codependent will do anything to avoid conflict, especially with the enabler.

Co-dependents and Narcissists

As you read about codependents and their tendencies, it should have become evident that codependents make the narcissist's ultimate target. They meet every line on the narcissist's agenda in choosing a target, and they are the ultimate victim. In a partnership between a codependent and a narcissist, the codependent gives endlessly to the narcissist, who needs the attention to feel loved. The narcissist gets to provide the codependent with the gift of being needed.

Both the narcissist and the codependent get their dysfunctional needs met. While this may seem like the perfect arrangement, it still encourages two people to live incredibly unhealthy lives. The codependent never has her basic needs met and still has broken self-esteem and lack of identity. The narcissist never gives back in the relationship and believes the narcissist is the only one who matters.

The narcissist's self-esteem and disordered thinking are not fixed through being catered to. This leads to an interesting relationship in which both the narcissist and the codependent enable each other.

Chapter 16:
Dealing with a Narcissist

There is no more fabulous teacher than personal experience and the knowledge and awareness that comes with it. Cutting all contact with the narcissist is the best possible scenario and speeds up the healing process. However, most of the time, relationships are not so simple, and there are other people or factors involved, such as children, colleagues, shared property, the workplace or family members. Of course, narcissists can the parents of our children, siblings, or bosses; in spite of the need to minimize contact, we are forced to have encounters with them, sometimes daily.

Awareness

When you are aware of their selfish behavior and have figured out their patterns, you can use this awareness to your advantage. Once you see through the narcissist and accept who they are, you can predict their reactions and use that knowledge to manipulate the situation in your favor. This does not mean becoming a narcissist yourself. It simply means protecting yourself from the abuser by knowing how they abuse you. You know the narcissist is up for what they can get, and you know they never change. What can change is your approach. Study your narcissist, observe them and spot the behavioral scheme you see. Knowing how they work and understanding that they are a self-serving person with a cluster B disorder, incapable of empathy, won't directly change how they treat you very much. What will change is how you perceive and react to them. This will minimize the mental and emotional damage they can inflict. Nothing they do is ever about you or anyone else; it is always about them. Knowing and accepting this and changing or enlightening them will save you from future hurt and giving in to their games.

Passivity and Disengagement

Covert narcissists are never mindful of your needs, so trying to explain your point of view, communicate your feelings, or seek understanding will only give them more material to manipulate you with. Don't try to seek justice or share with them; there is no space for compromise, tolerance, or a peaceful resolution unless it suits them at the moment. The best way to actively handle their blame games and gaslighting is to be aware of them and play along. For instance, when they blame you for being selfish, just tell them, you are right; I am so selfish. I agree with everything you say. If they are trying to convince you that you have done something you know you haven't, just play along. Oh yes, you are right; I remember I did that. This way, you turn their weapons, gaslighting and manipulation, against them, as they are perfectly aware, just like you are, that you never did what they accused you of. A narcissist is not a healthy individual, and this inauthentic act can protect you from being controlled by them. In the process, always be mindful of your actions and know who you are dealing with to protect your integrity.

You can also do this when you notice their behavior makes you feel heavyhearted or hurt, simply by disengaging and detaching yourself from the situation. Part of the disengagement technique includes self-discipline. When something feels off, don't try to find out why: just distance yourself from the situation. A narcissist communicates from an ego-centered place, and asking for explanations will only bring you more confusion and headache. Trust that the very feeling that something is not right is enough for you to leave the situation. Do so by acting peacefully and kindly, without explaining yourself, so as not to give the narcissist space to pull you back into their drama.

Privacy protection

You are dealing with an individual who is demanding a lot of mindfulness. What gives narcissists their power to control their targets is knowing their targets, predicting their behaviors and being aware of what makes them tick. That is why protecting yourself from narcissistic abuse in the future means keeping your life as private as possible. Don't let them know how you feel, what you fear or what you hope for. Distance yourself as much as possible and don't get them involved in your life. This will create a necessary barrier as they can't manipulate your feelings when they don't know what matters to you. Keep the narcissist informed only of fundamental things, such as moving locations when still sharing custody over children or keeping it strictly professional in the workplace.

Self-empowerment

In the end, there is nothing that defeats the narcissist more and protects you from them than having firm personal boundaries. This is something you will find easier to do by the end of the third stage of healing, so be patient. These skills are built slowly and require some practice. While not an easy road, fighting narcissistic abuse teaches us to protect ourselves and prioritize our needs once we know it.

Developing skills to cope with narcissism in others also includes practicing self-awareness, understanding and accepting your vulnerability without feeling flawed or weak. Being vulnerable means being human. Leave no space for someone to devalue you. Don't be afraid to say, no, when things don't feel right. There is no need to explain yourself, especially when dealing with a covert narcissist. Assert your boundaries calmly and don't feel bad for doing so. Saying no isn't selfish: it is healthy. The narcissist will probably try to pull you into their drama, so be aware of guilt-tripping and stay strong in your integrity. Trust yourself enough to walk away from things that don't feel good. It is ok and healthy to put yourself first. It is ok not to respond when you don't feel like it. Love is never restricting or conditional. Love is not abuse. Love feels good.

Being open to love, being giving and helpful are great virtues and should be cherished. These virtues will help you create balanced, healthy relationships in the future with a healthy individual who can reciprocate your love equally. Narcissists don't know how to appreciate it, and they give themselves permission to take it for granted and misuse it, which is not your fault. Not everyone is worthy of your love, and no one should cost you your peace of mind.

You are loveable and you are strong; otherwise, you wouldn't be here. And you are much more than you were told you are. One day, you will make it through. Life will be much different, and a narcissist won't cause you pain anymore. Once you get there, just remember to give yourself credit for it. Through adversity, we grow.

Chapter 17:
Your Road to Recovery

One of the things that you have to realize is that a narcissist does not see the need to seek help from a therapist because they think there is nothing wrong with them. Recovery is for those who have been through abuse. If you have been in a relationship with a narcissist, it is high time you left and sought help from a professional. This kind of support is needed to rebuild your self-confidence and bounce back to your former self-esteem.

Here are some of the steps you will have to go through on your journey through healing to recovery:

Step 1: Cut contact

Once you have left the relationship, keep it at that! Stop maintaining contact with your abuser. The main reason why you left is that the situation was not working for you. Nothing will happen that can make things better. The best way to recover from abuse is to block all forms of communication.

If you have joint custody of your children, you may not be able to wipe this person entirely from your life. Therefore, it is advisable to create a strict custom contract, according to which you only communicate on matters regarding your children using third-party channels exclusively! Otherwise, ensure that you have set up court orders for all forms of agreements.

Remember that you lived with them, and so the narcissist knows your weak points and how they can wound you even more profoundly. It is not until we heal that we will stop forcing ourselves on the narcissist for love or craving them - or even justifying giving them a second chance. When we completely stop contact, we can truly begin to heal.

Step 2: Release that trauma so that you begin functioning again

If we are going to heal, we have to be willing to reclaim our power. We have to do the exact opposite of what we used to believe, "I can fix him/her, I will feel better." Your power belongs inside you. The moment you take your focus away from your abuser, you will be able to channel that power into rebuilding your self-love and paying closer attention to making yourself whole again.

At first, it might seem like understanding who a narcissist is and what they do is essential. But the truth is that these things cannot heal your internal trauma. You need to decide to let go of that horrific experience so you can be at peace. You will begin to rise, get relief and rebalance once you have decided to take your power where it belongs - inside you.

Step 3: Forgive yourself for what you have been through

When the insecure and wounded parts of us are still in pain, we often are pushed into behaving like damaged children. We are constantly looking for people's approval, especially from our abuser. In fact, we hand our abuser the power to treat us as they see fit. And that's the time when you will realize that you have given them all your resources: money, time and health. The most unfortunate thing is that while doing that, you end up hurting the people that matter the most in your life...your children, siblings, parents, and friends.

You will realize that when you forgive yourself, you acknowledge that this was all a learning curve; hence, you will use the experience to reclaim your life. When you release your regrets and self-judgments, you can start setting yourself free to realize greatness in your life irrespective of what stage you are at. This is the point when you begin to feel hope again that will steer you forward and a life full of purpose.

Step 4: Release everything and heal all your fears of the abuser and what they might do next

Do you know what bait is to a narcissist? Anxiety, pain, and distress. These are the things that can perpetuate another cycle of abuse no matter how much we tell ourselves that we have separated from them. It is indeed true that abusers can be relentless. In most cases, they do not like being losers. They are not as powerful and impactful as you may have thought.

They need you to fear and go through pain to function. Once you have healed your emotional trauma, they fall apart. Therefore, you must become grounded and stoic by not feeding into their drama; this way, they will soon wither away along with their power and credibility.

Step 5: Release the connection to your abuser

So many people liken their freedom from a narcissist to that of exorcism. When we liberate ourselves from the darkness that filled our beings, we detox and let light and life come in. If that light has to take over the shade, the darkness has to leave to make space for something new to come in. In the same manner, you must release all the parts of you that were trapped by your abuser so you can tap into a more supernatural power - the power of pure creativity.

When you disentangle yourself from the narcissist, it is not just about cutting the cord; it is also about releasing all the belief systems you might have associated with subconsciously. It is only then that you can break free to be a new person and not a narcissist's target.

Even though it might be tempting to seek revenge on your abuser, this is something that you have to try hard to avoid. Rage has the power of pulling you back into deeper darkness and a game that your abuser is an expert at. The best form of revenge is the one in which you decide to take back your freedom and render your abuser irrelevant.

Step 6: Realize your liberation, truth, and freedom

Traditionally, we learn that loving ourselves is a very selfish act. However, when it comes to finding liberation from the hands of our abusers, the truth will set us free from captivity. Yes, it is challenging to do, but it is a necessary step toward freedom.

Society has taught us that we are treated by others the same way we treat them. However, this is a false premise because we are treated according to the way we treat ourselves. In other words, the measure of love we obtain from others is equivalent to what we feel about ourselves.

Therefore, when we open up to healing and recovery, we open the doors for others to love us in more healthy ways than ever before. This serves as a template by which we can teach our children not to carry around subconscious patterns of abuse passed on by our ancestors. This positive modeling only starts when we decide to take responsibility for our own happiness and freedom. We slowly see the change that we would wish to see when we let go of being someone's victim and stop handing other people our power.

So, what do you need to learn?

Refocus

One of the best things to learn from the whole experience is the danger of holding on to emotional attachments. When you let go, you experience the power that comes from healing. Take time to release those bond so you can refocus all your efforts on building a new life.

Self-confidence

If you want to live a life of greatness after your abuse, you must be willing to start putting your life back together. With self-confidence you can reclaim your old self and find an even higher power to steer you toward success and victory. Once you start experiencing self-love, you will be able to turn a chaotic life into one laden with calmness and joy.

Mindfulness

One of the things that you need to learn is to be fully present in the moment where your mind is not anxious about anything. It's the moment when you are calm and have clarity of thought. Only then that can you learn some of the powerful tools and tricks that will lead you to a life full of purpose and adventure.

Authenticity and integrity

The good thing for most survivors of abuse is the fact that they are often sincere. Their actions and words usually line up well. Through this extraordinary quality, you recognize your real personality and live a life doing good deeds for the entire society. Although these qualities are things to be proud of, you have to be willing to protect yourself, knowing that the person receiving your good deed is capable of reciprocating.

Establish new, robust, and healthy relationships

One of the best things you can learn from abuse is the art of connecting with new people in new ways. The best way is to attract healthy relationships with authentic friends who offer you a support system. Learn how to handle triggers, anxieties, fears, and stress. When you gain healthy relationship skills, you will be empowered to make better and more informed decisions in the future.

Accountability for your actions

Unfortunately, your narcissistic partner does not possess this gift; hence, their actions often make you feel more vulnerable. However, gaining your freedom from a narcissist allows you to fortify and reclaim your power when going into new relationships with the knowledge of how to set boundaries and getting people to respect them, no matter what. This will pave the way for healthier relationships filled with love and esteem, whether at the workplace, in your family, or your personal life.

Willingness to transition your relationships into mature and fundamental levels of intimacy

The good thing about surviving abuse is that you are empathetic. In other words, you learn what it takes to experience a healthy relationship filled with love and care for the other person. It is with this understanding that you can now exercise self-awareness. At some level, you know that the infatuation you have about the past will fade, and you will get back up on your horse and work on gaining true intimacy. You will be interested in truly knowing the other person well on a deeper, more personal level so you can unravel their real personality.

As a survivor, you are better equipped to move past your pain and abuse to a healthy relationship, whether in your family, workplace or love life. You can only do this with the right person, one who can reciprocate on the same deep level of emotional vulnerability and build complete trust.

Chapter 18:
Long-Term Recovery

Healing doesn't end even after the narcissist has been removed from your life. It is a process that takes an immeasurable amount of time. Nurturing your recovery will enable you to continue down the path of health and happiness. To ensure that you heal in the best way possible and the pain doesn't come back, I provide a few more practical steps. The recovery process needs to be continually nurtured. It's not a weekend program you do and never think about again. The emotional pain might subside, but there will still be bumps in the road. It is not a climb up a mountain but rather a ride on a rollercoaster. If you learn to anticipate the highs and lows, it will be much easier to stay in control of your emotional management as you ride along.

Breathing Exercises

Anyone dealing with anxiety can benefit from learning a few breathing exercises. This is the first place your mind should go when you start to feel overwhelmed and panicked. Breathing exercises are just as important when you are feeling happy as well. We often forget to focus on breathing, exacerbating the body's already panicked state when under intense stress. If you feel like texting your narcissistic ex, are triggered by your surroundings, or simply want to feel a bit more peace, try some of these exercises:

Alternate nose breathing - Take your right hand and place your pinky gently on your left nostril until it is closed. Breathe in through the right nostril. Hold it for a beat, then place your thumb on your right nostril in the same fashion as you remove your pinky from your left nostril. Slowly let the air out. Alternate your hands and nostrils as you feel yourself become more relaxed.

4-7-8 Breathing - Breathe in as you count to four. Hold it as you count to seven. Breathe out as you count to eight. Take a few seconds in between before doing this exercise again. You will feel the euphoria take over your brain. If you think too lightheaded, wait at least ten minutes before trying again.

Alternate nose-mouth breathing: Breathe in only through your nose as you count to five. Breathe out through a small hole in your mouth as you count to ten. This is a fundamental exercise whenever you are feeling scattered.

Mindfulness

Mindfulness is the best tool to keep you grounded. One thought can quickly turn into 1,000 ideas in an hour if you let yourself sit there and dwell on it. The mind is constantly active, so you can't just turn it off. Even in dreams, you might have to deal with memories of the narcissist!

Think of your thoughts like a snowball rolling down a hill. At first, you might not notice them, and maybe you don't even think they are a big deal, but as a thought keeps rolling, it collects more and more snow until it becomes so big it could roll right over a house! Stop your thoughts with mindfulness as soon as you notice them moving.

Try these mindful activities to help keep your mind calm:

Pick a color: Think of a random color—whatever comes to your mind first. Notice everything in the room of the same color. If you find your mind slipping back into anxious thoughts, find another color and repeat as needed until you can distract yourself further or refocus your attention where it needs to go.

Five senses: Once your mind starts racing, pull it back in your control by finding an object to correspond with each of your reasons. For sight, notice a luscious plant. For sound, maybe spot a guitar or

CD. For touch, identify something soft, rough, or textured. For smell, perhaps you notice a candle. For taste, you might pick out a candy dish. These things don't have to correspond with their obvious sense either. Think about what the leather couch smells like or what a houseplant tastes like. You don't have to do anything more than simply identify these things to keep your mind distracted.

Meditation

Meditation is like taking mindfulness to the next step. It involves refocusing your energy so your mind becomes completely blank. Search "guided meditation" on YouTube to find some beginner exercises if you are skeptical about meditation.

To begin, find a special place you can dedicate solely to meditative practices. This might include a sunroom, a backyard, or even a particular spot at the foot of your bed. Cleanse this space with sage to reset the energy. Sit in a comfortable position. You can sit in the classic meditative pose with the bottom of your feet placed together and your legs bent. You can also lie down with your eyes closed. Ensure you are in a comfy position that you won't want to move from repeatedly.

Start by focusing on your breathing. You can pick from any of the breathing exercises mentioned above. Pay attention to how your body feels as you breathe in and out. Notice any discomforts and try and relieve it from your body as you relax further.

As thoughts pass by, picture them as clouds. They will fade away and transform into shapes as you are lying there looking up at the sky. You can't grab them, you can't hold them, you can't change them. Just let them float away. Pay them no mind. They will keep coming, but you will keep letting them simply fade away.

Meditating can be hard for beginners. You might find that your mind is continually going back to scattered thoughts. New anxieties and big fears might come in like a blaring alarm. Remember to center back on your breathing. You don't have to give in to these thoughts or do anything with them. There is no urgency for reflection. The most important part of meditation is to clear your mind so you can reset your thoughts.

Creating

Creating anything can be incredibly fulfilling. Not everyone will be the next Picasso, but freely expressing yourself will help you become more comfortable. Finishing a craft project like a knitted scarf or refurbished chair can boost your self-esteem and give you something to be proud of.

Explore different creative avenues and find something you feel comfortable with. Try oil paints, acrylics, or watercolors. Try sketching with pencils, chalk, or even crayons. Get messy. Get crazy. Get excited!

Creativity extends beyond the art store as well. Try new recipes and cook something you haven't before. Follow a recipe verbatim. Make homemade salad dressing, cocktails, bread, and other things you've never tried.

Get creative with your space. Rearrange the furniture, buy new decorations, and try a style you haven't thought of. Start gardening or buy a houseplant. You have been shackled and abused by the narcissist in your life for so long that it might feel strange to do something for yourself, but exploring that side of you can be just the remedy needed to make a full recovery.

Changing Lifestyles

If there is ever a time to start a new lifestyle, now is the time! Is there something you have wanted to do for a while? Maybe you want to make a career switch. Perhaps you're interested in going back to school. You might just try veganism or at least eat a nutritious, plant-based diet. Starting something completely new can give you the exact fresh perspective that is needed. Rearranging your bedroom or painting your kitchen can make this fresh start feel more realistic.

Make sure you are doing this for yourself because you want to and not just because you think you should. The point of making lifestyle changes is to replace bad habits with better ones. If you already enjoy your life, you don't necessarily have to change it; now is just a good time to do so if you have already been wishing for a drastic change.

Support Systems

Find new sources of support wherever you can. It's straightforward for those recovering from trauma to turn to dangerous or unhealthy vices when seeking to numb that emotional pain. Those who have lived through trauma are more likely to turn to drug or alcohol abuse. They might end up in dangerous situations and experience harmful behavior because of small choices that lead to a negative chain of events.

Maintain support even when you are feeling healthier. Although you might think you've made a full recovery and you're ready to face your most giant demons, you could end up getting triggered. If the support system isn't there, it can be easy to fall back into harmful habits.

Support can start simply online. You can open an anonymous account on a forum site like Reddit to meet like-minded people. You can take it further and look for group therapy. Don't ever be afraid to ask for help and support. You not only need it—you deserve it.

Continued Growth

Growth takes time. You don't plant seeds and expect flowers to bloom the next day. You don't give birth and hope the baby to feed itself right away. Growth is also like a roller coaster. Sometimes there are quick bursts and a lot of change happens. Occasionally, you will dip back into old habits. Sometimes the growth is slow and steady.

Never stop nourishing your desire for growth. As humans, we are constantly changing. Even though our minds stop developing after adulthood, that doesn't mean they stop changing forever. There are always transformations, epiphanies, and moments of enlightenment ahead.

You might never hit a point where you can say, "I'm completely healed from my abuse, and the trauma doesn't affect me anymore." It might stay with you forever. But this isn't a bad thing at all! You will eventually realize that your trauma is simply a scar that has helped develop you into the person you are now. You've lived through tough things, and that means you will come out even stronger afterwards.

Always look for ways to let yourself grow, be free, and become the person you are meant to be. If anyone ever tries to stop that from happening, you know exactly how to handle it now.

Conclusion

A Healthy life with a narcissist is impossible. They do not know how to communicate with others in a way that is not manipulative. This is likely because as a child, they could not get their needs met by asking and had to go about it in an underhanded way. Then and as an adult, they continue this behavior. They will likely use stories of childhood tragedies as a way of playing on your sympathy and getting you not to leave them. You can feel compassion for what they endured as a child, but you owe it to yourself not to tolerate abuse from the person they have become as an adult.

This means their time needs to be filled with something else, so they won't have time to think about and contact the person they are trying to distance themselves from. This is the time to make new friends and reconnect with old ones.

A person who is a victim of long-term narcissistic abuse needs some form of psychiatric care because, at this point, they are also mentally unwell. They have likely regressed into a state of learned helplessness and have cultivated a victim mentality. They do not think they can do anything about their situation. They have developed a trauma bond with the narcissist, a term used to describe a victim's psychology repeatedly going back to their abuser. Partially it is because they do not think they deserve better, and they also have the idea of "it's better to live with the evil you do know than face the unknown." This is a thought process they will have to break to escape the cycle of abuse.

Cognitive-behavioral therapy, also known as CBT, is highly effective in treating a person trying to recover from narcissistic abuse. A therapist who practices CBT guides their patients by taking negative thinking patterns that are destructive to one's mental health and transforming them into more positive ones.

The trauma bond is a distorted thinking pattern. The narcissistic abuse victim has become addicted to the positively emotionally charged cycle of their relationship with the narcissist. There are several reasons for this. Constant putdowns have torn down their self-esteem. The narcissist also knows exactly how much abuse their victim can take and when they have to use the love-bombing tactics again.

This creates a feeling that the connection between them is more profound than the ones they had with other people in the past because the two of them have "been through so much." The victim also might have been raised by a narcissist, so they are subconsciously gravitating toward what is familiar.

This is why the narcissist must take up a hobby and do something productive to meet new people. Their past abuser's insults have become a voice in their head, and this voice needs to be eliminated.

For example, if they take up sewing, they will feel a sense of accomplishment when they have created a piece of clothing, which will automatically boost their self-esteem. It will also develop friendships with people who think well of them and show them affection.

Their kind words will eventually challenge the negative ones from their abuser, and ultimately, the thought will cross the person's mind, "should I listen to one person who doesn't like me, or all of these other people who do?"

While this means blocking the victim, you could contact them, but ignore the barrage of calls and messages that will soon follow. You may have the urge to get them again and begin the smear campaign that so many narcissists throw upon their victims when they attempt to leave.

A covert narcissist is exceptionally skilled at starting a smear campaign. They have carefully crafted an image of themselves as helpless victims, and they enjoy assassinating someone else's character. The narcissist will tell others they do not know you as well as they think they do. They will try to convince everyone that you are mentally unstable while masking the mental instability that drives them to do this to yet another person. If you remain unresponsive, everyone will see you as being calm and collected while they are ranting and raving about you. Eventually, no one will want to hear them talk about you anymore.

It is a good idea to connect with people who have shared your experiences. The right group will hold you accountable and talk you out of making mistakes - like breaking the rule of no contact. They will not excuse you. A support group's goal should be to help one another move on, not stay in the same unhappy place.

If you must talk to the person because of children, work, or some other reason, use the tactic known as grey rocking. This technique has its name because the goal is to be as emotionless and uninterested as a grey rock.

CPSIA information can be obtained
at www.ICGtesting.com
Printed in the USA
BVHW090851260421
605871BV00002B/330

9 781914 527135